DATE DUE			

SOURCES FOR SOCIAL AND ECONOMIC HISTORY

The Factory System

VOLUME II: THE FACTORY SYSTEM AND SOCIETY

SOURCES FOR SOCIAL AND ECONOMIC HISTORY

J. T. WARD

Senior Lecturer in Economic History
University of Strathclyde

The Factory System

VOLUME II: THE FACTORY SYSTEM AND SOCIETY

BARNES & NOBLE, Inc.

NEW YORK

PUBLISHERS & BOOKSELLERS SINCE 1873

338.65
W21f
7 6306
Nov. 1971
V. 2

COPYRIGHT NOTICE

First published in the United States, 1970
by Barnes & Noble, Inc.

ISBN 389-04044-4

Printed in Great Britain

Contents

              page

INTRODUCTION   11

PART ONE: THE CONSEQUENCES OF THE FACTORY SYSTEM

Artisans and Machinery   18

1 Peter Gaskell. *Artisans and Machinery* (1836)   18

2 Richard Guest. *A Compendious History of the Cotton Manufacture,* (1823)   22

3 Charles Babbage. *On the Economy of Machinery and Manufactures* (1832)   24

Industrial Health   26

4 Charles Turner Thackrah. *The Effects of Arts, Trades and Professions . . . on Health and Longevity* (1832)   27

5 Robert Baker. *The Present Condition of the Working Classes* (Bradford, 1851)   30

The Factory Town   31

6 Ernest Jones. 'The Factory Town' (1847)   32

7 John James. *The History of Bradford* (1866)   34

8 William Cooke Taylor. *Notes of a Tour in the Manufacturing Districts of Lancashire* (1842)   37

9 John Jones. *The Cotton Mill* (Manchester, 1821)   41

10 Benjamin Disraeli, *Sybil, or the Two Nations* (1845)   42

5

Factory Life *page* 44

11 Michael Thomas Sadler. 'The Factory Girl's Last Day' (1832) 44

12 Alexander Thomson. *Random Notes and Rambling Recollections of . . . Maryhill* (Glasgow, 1895) 46

13 [James Myles]. *Chapters in the Life of a Dundee Factory Boy* (Dundee, 1850) 48

Visits to the Factories 56

14 [Louis Simond]. *Journal of a Tour and Residence in Great Britain* (Edinburgh, 1815) 57

15 Frances Trollope. *The Life and Adventures of Michael Armstrong* (1840) 60

16 William Cooke Taylor. *Notes of a Tour in the Manufacturing Districts of Lancashire* (1842) 62

PART TWO: FACTORY REFORM

Child Labour 67

17 Gilbert J. French. *The Life and Times of Samuel Crompton* (Manchester, 1859) 67

18 Report of Minutes of Evidence respecting the state of health and morals of Children employed in Manufactories (1816) 68

19 Report from the Select Committee on . . . the Labour of Children in the Mills and Factories (1832) 71

The Leadership of Richard Oastler 73

20 *Leeds Mercury* (1830) 73

21 *Leeds Intelligencer* and *Leeds Patriot* (1831) 76

22 *The Home* (1852) 79

23 *The Fleet Papers* (1841) 80

The Factory Reformers   *page* 82

24 William Busfeild Ferrand. 'Letters to the Duke of Newcastle' (1852)   82

25 *Ashton and Stalybridge Reporter* (1858)   83

26 *Manchester and Salford Advertiser* (1835)   85

27 *Protest of the Rev. G. S. Bull* (Bradford, 1833)   88

The Ten Hours Bill   91

28 [Samuel Kydd]. *The History of the Factory Movement* (1857)   92

29 *Memoirs of the Life and Writings of Michael Thomas Sadler*
(1842)   99

30 Geoffrey Crabtree. *Factory Commission* (1833)   103

31 *Great Meeting in Leeds* (Leeds, 1833)   104

32 [Samuel Kydd]. *The History of the Factory Movement* (1857)   105

33 First Report from the Commissioners appointed to collect
information in the Manufacturing Districts (1833)   106

The Factory Reform Agitation   108

34 Richard Oastler. *Facts and Plain Words* (Leeds, 1833)   108

35 Richard Oastler. *Speech delivered in . . . Bradfurd* (*Leeds,*
1833)   112

36 *Resolutions of the Society for Promoting National Regeneration*
(Manchester, 1833)   114

37 Richard Oastler. *A Letter to . . . The Bradford Observer* (Bradford, 1834)   115

38 Richard Oastler. *The Unjust Judge* (Leeds, 1836)   116

39 Joseph Rayner Stephens. *A Sermon preached . . . at Charlestown* (1839)   118

The Propaganda Battle   120

40 John Fielden. *The Curse of the Factory System* (1836)   120

41 Charles Wing. *Evils of the Factory System demonstrated* (1837) 124

42 Leonard Horner. *On the Employment of Children* (1840)   126

43 *The Factory Bill* (Pudsey, 1836)   129

The Later Movement   *page* 132

44 Lord Ashley to the Short Time Committees (1842)   132

45 Joseph Vickers. 'Ten Hours' Factory Labour' (Keighley,
1844)   133

46 Henry Green, Matthew Balme. 'The Ten Hours' Bill'
(Manchester, 1845)   134

47 Lord Ashley to the Short Time Committees (1846)   135

48 *The Champion* 'Ryder v Mills' (1850)   137

PART THREE: THE FACTORY SYSTEM AND
            SOCIETY

The Masters' Case   140

49 Joseph Birley. *Sadler's Bill. Cotton Branch* (Manchester,
1832)   141

50 *A Letter to Sir John Cam Hobhouse* (1832)   141

51 Vernon Royle. *The Factory System defended* (Manchester,
1833)   142

52 Robert Hyde Greg. *The Factory Question* (1837)   143

The 'Intellectual' Attitude   146

53 Nassau W. Senior. *Letters on the Factory Act* (1837)   146

54 Andrew Ure. *The Philosophy of Manufactures* (1835)   152

55 Francis Place. 'Handloom Weavers and Factory Workers'
(1835)   157

56 Edward Baines. *The Manufacturing Districts Vindicated*
(Leeds, 1843)   158

The Operation of Factory Legislation   161

57 *Leeds Intelligencer* (1838)   161

58 *Leeds Mercury* (1848)   163

59 Reports on the Effects of the Educational Provisions of the
Factories Act (1839)   164

60 Report of Factory Inspector Thomas Jones Howell (1841) 166

61 'An Act to Amend the Laws Relating to Labour in Fac- *page*
tories' (1844)   166

Working-Class Organisations   167

62 Frank Peel. *The Risings of the Luddites, Chartists and Plugdrawers* (Heckmondwike, 1888)   168

63 First Report of the Select Committee on Combinations of
Workmen (1838)   168

64 Thomas Cooper. *The Life of Thomas Cooper* (1872)   170

65 *The Lancaster Trials* (1843)   171

Changing Views on the Factory System   172

66 *Speeches of the Right Honorable T. B. Macaulay* (1854)   172

67 *The Manchester Guardian* (1847, 1850)   180

68 Robert Baker. *The Factory Acts Made Easy* (Leeds, 1854)   182

69 Robert Baker. 'On the Physical Effects of Diminished
Labour' (1859)   182

70 Sir Edwin Hodder. *The Life and Work of the Seventh Earl of
Shaftesbury, K.G.* (1886)   184

Industry's Triumph   186

71 *The Times* (1851)   187

NOTES   188

INDEX   195

Introduction

'We are living at a period of most wonderful transition, which tends rapidly to accomplish that great end, to which, indeed all history points—*the realization of the unity of mankind*', declared the Prince Consort in 1850. 'The distances which separated the different nations and parts of the globe are rapidly vanishing before the achievements of modern invention . . . [and] the *great principle of division of labour*, which may be called the moving power of civilization, is being extended to all branches of science, industry and art'. The Prince undoubtedly voiced feelings widely held in mid-century Britain. The classic period of the Industrial Revolution was yielding to Britain's age as the Workshop of the World. Frugality, self-help, hard work and constant reinvestment appeared to be paying-off. Bourgeois villas were creating suburbs round every industrial city. The archetype of the relatively prosperous, politically moderate, respectable and respectful Victorian artisan was appearing with the new concept of an aristocracy of labour. Above all, peaceful co-operation in trade and industry seemed to be guaranteed by the hoped-for extension of universal free trade. 'The cause of free trade is the cause of *civil liberty* . . . the cause of *political justice*', Philip Harwood told the London Mechanics Institution in 1843. 'The cause of free trade is the cause of *peace*; peace at home and peace abroad; peace between class and class, and between nation and nation.'

The optimism of the mid-century had many features and much to support it, as Joseph Paxton's vast Crystal Palace rose in Hyde Park for the Great Exhibition of the Industry of all

Nations in 1851. George Porter and a host of others proudly published the statistical evidence of industrial growth. Raw cotton consumption had risen from 52,000,000 lb in 1800 to 630,000,000 lb in 1849. By 1850 the cotton industry directly employed 331,000 factory workers and 43,000 handloom weavers; the woollen, worsted, and shoddy industries had 154,000 factory workers; the flax, hemp and jute industries 68,000; and the silk industry 43,000.[1] Steam power had revolutionised factory industry, transport, and society itself. The results were a marvel to the world. 'To reach Manchester standards of efficiency in Swiss factories', wrote Hans Escher even in 1814, 'we should have to sack all our operatives and train up a new generation of apprentices'.

There was an additional moral bonus to be derived from clothing mankind. 'What a delight it is in going to the Holy City to stop with the caravan at Nazareth—to see four thousand individuals, and scarcely be able to fix upon one to whom your country has not presented some comfort or decoration!', exclaimed John Bowring in 1838. 'Peace and industry have been doing this and much more. . . .' The same Bowring was to preach a harsher free-trade doctrine to Chinese officials trying to put down smuggling in the late 1850s. But Richard Cobden, the Stockport industrialist whose contribution to free trade was such that the hardest-headed Manchester businessmen had subscribed to his testimonial fund, had explained the virtues of peaceful competition throughout Europe; and in this increasingly bourgeois age his followers had regularly contended that wars were aristocratic inventions. 'The very language of monopoly savours of war', asserted Harwood. 'The whole monopoly argument bristles with jealousy, suspicion and enmity. . . .' The effete feudal noblemen, with their coats-of-arms and their rustic retainers, were a warlike crowd, but the new masters—the self-made, politically and theologically dissenting men of the mill,

---

[1] These and many other statistics are conveniently collected together in B. R. Mitchell and Phyllis Deane, *Abstract of British Historical Statistics*, ch 7. Cambridge, 1962.

the exchange, and the shippers' office—would inaugurate a new era of peaceful development; yet two years after the Exhibition the lancers, dragoons, hussars, and their kind were shipped off to the Crimea to fight the last of their wars.

The campaign over the repeal of the Corn Laws had been fought partly (and rather unfairly) in terms of a class war between reactionary landowners and liberal factory owners. 'Monopoly may be rich in dukes, but it is poor in thinkers—its hosts number many squires and justices of the quorum; but they are miserably ill off for philosophers', sneered Harwood. Certainly the new rich resented the power, privilege, and prestige of ancient wealth. 'Industry now stood side by side with hereditary opulence', wrote Henry Dunckley in 1854. 'The owner of ten thousand spindles confronted the lord of ten thousand acres. . . .' But the contrast between the two wealthy classes is exaggerated. The 'open' British peerage, small as it was, was no Continental aristocracy. Its members were not afraid to soil their hands with industrial ventures or their blood by bourgeois marriages. Furthermore, the system of primogeniture had ensured that their younger sons had for centuries sought their livelihood away from the land. The successful manufacturer quickly became a landowner himself. Victorian social registers record the descent, country seats, and armorial bearings of such newcomers as Arkwright, Strutt, Peel, Cunliffe-Lister, Wood, Marshall, Monteith, Fielden, and Edwards. The new public schools polished their sons into replicas of an only recently polished country gentry.

The old romanticism of Church and State had enjoyed a brief resurrection in the Gothic revival. This protest against the times took many forms: for example, Pugin's architecture, Scott's novels, Lord Eglinton's tragi-comic medieval 'tournament', the Tractarians' revival of Catholic theology and liturgical practices, the paternalist politics of the 'Young England' Tories, and the heraldic fantasies conjured up by the genealogists. Such interest influenced the new men in differents ways. Some added 'Gothick' motifs to their mills and factories or built mock-baronial villas in industrial suburbs and castellated mansions in the country. Others thought industry romantic. Even Disraeli's 'Young Englanders' had sensed a dramatic power in the Manchester of 1844, which had 'dethroned Force and placed on her high seat Intelligence'. More committed men could see even greater virtues in industry. 'Trade has now a chivalry of its own', declared Dunckley, 'a chivalry whose stars are radiant with the more benignant lustre of justice, happiness, and religion, and whose titles will outlive the barbarous nomenclature of Charlemagne'. There was, first of all, a feeling of wonder at recent technological success. 'In whatever light we examine the triumphs and achievements of our species over the creation submitted to its power', wrote Professor Charles Babbage in 1832, 'we explore new sources of wonder'. Secondly, there was the excitement of prediction; nothing seemed impossible to the world's first industrial nation. Erasmus Darwin was one of many who ventured to forecast the future in 1792:

> Soon shall thy arm, UNCONQUER'D STEAM! afar
> Drag the slow barge, or drive the rapid car;
> Or on wide-waving wings expanded bear
> The flying-chariot through the fields of air.

But above all, mid-century Victorians could rejoice in their achievement. The slummy mill-towns, the smoking chimneys, the glaring furnaces, the towering slagheaps, and the railways' desecration of the quiet countryside might now offend and even anger many poets and 'sentimentalists'; but such different men as Dr Arnold, who rejoiced at the passing of 'feudality' on seeing the first train reach Rugby, and Ebenezer Elliott, the Sheffield 'corn law rhymer', could appreciate and praise the social changes wrought by industry. One might have 'social' concern, but still be impressed by the technological achievement. The radical Elliott explained the sentiment:

> Oh, there is glorious harmony in this
> Tempestuous music of the giant, Steam,

Commingling growl, and roar, and stamp, and hiss,
With flame and darkness!

As British workers, backed by British capital, used British machines to produce British goods which were to be exported all over the world in British ships, mid-century Britons could well feel proud of past achievement and sanguine about the future. They were entitled also to credit for revolutionising industry without provoking a social revolution—though, on occasion, it had been 'a damned close thing'. They had provided work for a rapidly growing population for most of the time, and a gradually improving standard of living, at least after the early bleak years of the Industrial Revolution. They created the first urban industrial civilisation, and were not afraid to spend their money—on houses and pleasures, on new factories, on the world's first railways, on the largely reluctant maintenance and extension of an empire which only became briefly a matter of pride to their grandchildren, and on the extension of Christian missions at home and abroad.

The new wealth created by industry ultimately led to more compassion in society; but despite its concern for negro slaves in America and Africa, its interest in every variety of sectarian religion, and its preoccupation with an increasingly puritanical morality, early Victorian Britain tolerated many abuses. The old brutal sports involving cruelty to animals were slowly dying out, but small boys dying of cancer swept Britain's chimneys, women and children hauled its coal along underground corridors, thousands of boys and girls worked long hours in the mills and factories, and practitioners of ancient hand crafts fought desperately against starvation. *Laisser-faire* was never adopted as State policy—as the old restrictive laws fell into disuse or were abolished, a new type of state interference was evolved— but it was the philosophy of the age. Consequently, successive reformers, seeking to invoke a paternalist (or sometimes socialist) *étatisme*, faced bitter hostility. Men must be encouraged to care for themselves. At the best, they might receive charity from one of the numerous voluntary societies (whose functions ranged from suppressing vice to promoting proletarian cleanliness); and at the worst, for the incapable, the old, the orphaned, the unemployed, there was the grim forbidding workhouse.

The following pages contain a selection of contemporary views on the factory system, and concentrate upon the factory's social consequences. An attempt has been made to balance both the viewpoints expressed and the amount of well known and lesser known material. With its companion volume on the birth and growth of the factory system, it is offered as a contribution to the study of a seminal period of industrial history.

PART ONE

The Consequences of the Factory System

The development of the factory system between 1815 and 1847 increased production by 3·5 per cent annually. Textiles—particularly the cotton industry, which by 1851 employed some 527,000 workers—made a major contribution to this growth. In 1815 cotton accounted for 40 per cent of British exports and in 1830 over 50 per cent. By 1841 83 per cent of English cotton workers were employed in factories, as against 44·1 per cent of woollen workers. Although traditional occupations, largely unaffected by the Industrial Revolution, still dominated mid-century employment, the 5 per cent of the working population employed in textiles provided the bulk of exports and constituted a new 'class'. Contemporary commentators often admired the achievements of the new industries. But many workers faced new social problems: increased earnings were balanced by the break-up of the family, long hours by periodic unemployment, increased opportunities by the redundancy or long decline of older craftsmen. Doctors catalogued the diseases and injuries common in various occupations and pioneer sociologists reported on the state of the new factory towns. Class antagonisms developed; in 1844 Leon Faucher found that 'there was nothing but masters and operatives' in Manchester; and industrial life and labour were often hard and brutish. On the other hand, factory-dominated textiles stimulated other industries (such as engineering and transport), contributed to town growth, clothed a large

part of the world's population, created many middle-class fortunes, and established Britain's rôle as the world's workshop.

Artisans and Machinery   Peter Gaskell (1806–41), a liberal-
minded surgeon, published two celebrated accounts of industrial
life and labour in the 1830s. He generally struck a middle course
in the argument over working conditions, discounting the
'wilder' allegations but still insisting that much was wrong with
the system. After practising in Camberwell, he moved to the
cotton town of Stockport and thereafter wrote on the basis of
'extensive personal research and inquiry'. In 1833 he maintained that factory children 'have pale and flaccid features, a
stunted growth, very often tumid bellies, tender eyes, and other
marks that the *primae viae* have been permitted to go wrong'. To
him, 'factory labour was a species of work, in some respects
singularly unfitted for children'; but parents, as well as factory
owners, were responsible for the children's ill-health.

1   The Factory Commissioners visited the factory districts at a
time when the public mind had been filled with the most fearful
details of the cruelty and profligacy existing in them; and on
finding that many of these details were gross exaggerations, and
that in some mills an admirable system of physical and moral
discipline had been established, they have gone to the opposite
side of the question, and consequently are as much in error, on
points of opinion, as many of the theoretical witnesses examined
before Mr. Sadler's Committee in 1833.

. . . Committees of the House of Commons have, at different
periods, examined into some of the points of this inquiry. It
happens, however, unfortunately, that the evidence given before these Committees, and the reports founded upon that
evidence, are looked at suspiciously, and have in effect little
weight or consideration . . .*

*Witness the Committee of the House of Commons in 1832, of which Mr.
Sadler was chairman. The mildest term which the evidence before that
Committee deserves is, that it is full of extravagances. [The date given
supra was incorrect.]

... The greatest misfortune—the most unfavourable change which has resulted from factory labour—is the breaking up of these family ties, the consequent abolition of the domestic circle, and the perversion of all the social obligations which should exist between parent and child on the one hand, and between children themselves on the other. ...

Factory labour, in many of its processes, requires little else but manual dexterity, and no physical strength; neither is there anything for the mind to do in it; so that children, whose fingers are taught to move with great facility and rapidity, have all the requisites for it. Hence one reason for introducing these infants into mills, though this is by no means the only one; and were the hours of labour sufficiently limited, and under proper regulation, when the present habits of their parents are considered, the evil—great in some respects as it is—would almost cease to be one. Children from nine to twelve years of age are now become part of the staple hands, and are consequently subjected at this tender period to all the mischiefs incident to the condition of the older work-people.*

... The houses of great numbers of the labouring community in the manufacturing districts are filthy, unfurnished, and deprived of all the accessories to decency or comfort ...

The bringing together numbers of the young of both sexes in factories, has been a prolific source of moral delinquency. The stimulus of a heated atmosphere, the contact of opposite sexes, the example of license upon the animal passions—all have conspired to produce a very early development of sexual appetencies. Indeed, in this respect, the female population engaged in mill labour, approximates very closely to that found in tropical climates; puberty, or at least sexual propensities, being attained almost coeval with womanhood ... [The manufacturer] considers the human beings who crowd his mill, from five o'clock in the morning to seven o'clock in the evening, but as so many

* The "Factories Regulation Act" has caused multitudes of these children to be dismissed, but it has only increased the evils it was intended to remedy, and must of necessity be repealed.

accessories to his machinery, destined to produce a certain and well-known quantity of work, at the lowest possible outlay of capital. To him their passions, habits, or crimes, are as little interesting as if they bore no relation to the errors of a system, of which he was a member and supporter.

. . . Nothing appearing then in the condition of the labour, considered *per se*, to which children are subjected, of an actively injurious character, as far as physical health is concerned, the evils, if any, have their origin in cases foreign to it,—and these are, first, its continuance, and secondly, the prevention of all recreation and exercise necessary for sustaining or repairing their already shattered constitutions: and to these must be added the moral effects of example, of independent earning and appropriation of wages . . .

. . . The employment of children in manufactories ought not to be looked upon as an evil till the present moral and domestic habits of the population are completely reorganized. So long as home education is not found for them, they are to some extent better situated when engaged in light labour, and the labour generally is light which falls to their share. The duration of mill labour, from the natural state of the body during growth, and where there is a previous want of healthy development, is too long.

. . . The real evil lies in the habits of the people themselves; habits, it is very true, generated by the system of factory labour: and one half the mischiefs suffered by the children are inflicted upon them prior to the commencing work . . .

The attempts made by the Poor Law Commissioners to encourage the depressed agriculturalists to emigrate into the manufacturing districts, is at once strange and unaccountable, and can only serve to derange the present trembling balance which connects the human labourer to many mill processes, and to lower the value of labour generally, at a crisis when such a process will be dangerous to the prospects of that vast branch of industry dependent upon manufactures . . .

. . . Few amongst the population can be said to enjoy perfect health; all are more or less ailing, and are deprived of every chance of restoration by the impossibility of removing themselves from the influence which is ever around and within them.

. . . Labour being the poor man's sole possession, his property, deserves an equal portion of legislative protection with property of any other kind; and in return it should be content to be placed under the same restraints and regulations, which are placed for the benefit of all parties upon other kinds of property . . .

Nothing should be expected from the master-manufacturer beyond this—that he should not enrich himself at the expense of his labourers; but after securing that which he has a right to do—a proper return for his outlay of capital, risk, and other contingencies, then that surplus should be considered due to the labourers, and paid over to them in such a way as to interfere the least with their independent use of it . . .

These [industrial] struggles have uniformly been most disastrous to the men, and must ever be so. It is in vain that in their rage, worked up into madness by heartless demagogues, by hunger, by the sight of their famishing children, they have taken the law into their own hands, and dreadful proofs have they given how unfit were they to wield it for their own benefit. Incendiarism, machine breaking, assassination, vitriol throwing, acts of diabolical outrage, all have been perpetrated for intimidation or revenge; but in all cases with the like result, or when partial success has attended them, it has been but temporary.

The extent to which combinations exist amongst workmen is only fully shewn when a general strike in a particular branch of trade takes place. Then they are seen ramifying in every direction, embracing all trades alike, each having their separate rules and code of laws, but all uniting in one point, to support the operative, when he either voluntarily abstracts himself from employ, or is driven out by some new demand on the part of his master. Each trade has a sort of corporate board for the management of its funds, the protection so called of its particular interests, and this board is paid for its services out of a specific

allowance made by every workman who is a member of the
union or combination. The sums thus abstracted from the
pockets of the deluded artisan have been very considerable, the
regulations being compulsory in the extreme.

. . . Combinations of workmen against masters—of labour
against capital—have uniformly, in the manufacturing districts,
been injurious to the men to a much greater extent than to the
master.

. . . The general combinations, which include nearly the
whole of the manufacturing population, and which are so
mischievous in their effects, have numerous minor and sub-
sidiary co-operative unions. The spinners, weavers, piecers,
finishers, &c. &c., each combine in their own class, and have
each distinct rules and regulations for their direction; subordi-
nate, however, to the general confederations into which their
distinct interests merge . . . They are . . . quite distinct in their
separate corporate capacities, acting quite independently of
one another, and assimilating only in being parties in the
general combination. Peter Gaskell. *Artisans and Machinery: The
Moral and Physical Condition of the Manufacturing Population considered with reference to Mechanical Substitutes for Human Labour*, ix,
1–2, 61, 66–7, 78, 103, 104, 162, 164–5, 166, 172, 231, 262, 264,
268–9, 276, 277–8. 1836

————

Many observers agreed that the advent of new industrial tech-
niques initially improved the general level of intelligence of
former rural workers. Richard Guest here describes the change
wrought among cotton workers by increasing concentration and
by the Sunday School movement, dominated from 1780 by
Robert Raikes (1735–1811).

————

2 The progress of the cotton manufacture introduced great
changes in the manners and habits of the people. The operative
workmen being thrown together in great numbers, had their
faculties sharpened and improved by constant communication.
Conversation wandered over a variety of topics not before

essayed; the questions of peace and war, which interested them importantly, inasmuch as they might produce a rise or fall of wages, became highly interesting, and this brought them into the vast field of politics and discussions on the character of their Government, and the men who composed it. They took a greater interest in the defeats and victories of their country's arms, and from being only a few degrees above their cattle in the scale of intellect, they became Political Citizens.

To these changes the establishing of Sunday Schools has very much contributed; they have been a great means of forwarding this wonderful alteration. Before their institution the lower orders were extremely illiterate; very few of them could read, and still fewer could write, and when one of them learned to read, write and cast accounts, those acquirements elevated him to a superior rank. His clerkly skill exempted him from manual labour, and as a shopman, book-keeper or town's officer—perchance in the higher dignity of parish clerk or schoolmaster—he rose a step above his original situation in life.

The labourers and operative workmen were formerly sunk in the depths of ignorance; they seldom formed an opinion of their own, and were content to believe everything their superiors told them. Sunday Schools have greatly assisted in dispelling this cloud of ignorance, they have taught the mass of the people to read, and the countless publications dispersed over the country, in monthly portions or numbers, at 6d. 9d. or 1s. per number, have taught them to reason and think for themselves. During the last 40 years the mind of the labouring class (taking them as a body) has been progressively improving, and within the last 20, has made an advance of centuries, and is still advancing with accelerated rapidity.

The facility with which the weavers changed their masters, the constant effort to find out and obtain the largest remuneration for their labour, the excitement to ingenuity which the higher wages for fine manufactures and skilful workmanship produced, and a conviction that they depended mainly on their own exertions, produced in them that invaluable feeling, a spirit of freedom and independence, and that guarantee for good conduct and improvement of manners, a consciousness of the value of character and of their own weight and importance. Richard Guest. *A Compendious History of the Cotton Manufacture*, 37–8. 1823

An inevitable result of factory production and mechanisation of production processes was unemployment or a long battle between handworkers and factory industry. The weavers, in particular, tried to compete with the factories' powered machines but failed. In the following extract Charles Babbage (1792–1871), mathematician, mechanic and Lucasian Professor of Mathematics at Cambridge in 1828–39, presents a liberal explanation of such problems. First published in 1832, his book was often reissued.

3 One of the objections most frequently urged against machinery is, that it has a tendency to supersede much of the hand-labour which was previously employed; and in fact unless a machine diminished the labour necessary to make an article, it could never come into use. But if it have that effect, its owner, in order to extend the sale of his produce, will be obliged to undersell his competitors; this will induce them also to introduce the new machine, and the effect of this competition will soon cause the article to fall, until the profits on capital, under the new system, shall be reduced to the same rate as under the old. Although, therefore, the use of machinery has at first a tendency to throw labour out of employment, yet the increased demand consequent upon the reduced price, almost immediately absorbs a considerable portion of that labour, and perhaps, in some cases, the whole of what would otherwise have been displaced.

That the effect of a new machine is to diminish the labour required for the production of the *same* quantity of manufactured commodities may be clearly perceived, by imagining a society, in which occupations are not divided, each man manufacturing all the articles he consumes. Supposing each individual to labour during ten hours daily, one of which is devoted to making shoes, it is evident that if any tool or machine be introduced, by the use of which his shoes can be made in half the usual time, then each member of the community will enjoy the same comforts as before by only nine and one-half hours' labour.

If, therefore, we wish to prove that the total quantity of labour is not diminished by the introduction of machines, we must have recourse to some other principle of our nature. But the same motive which urges a man to activity will become additionally powerful, when he finds his comforts procured with diminished labour; and in such circumstances, it is probable, that many would employ the time thus redeemed in contriving new tools for other branches of their occupations . . .

In countries where occupations are divided, and where the division of labour is practised, the ultimate consequence of improvements in machinery is almost invariably to cause a greater demand for labour. Frequently the new labour requires, at its commencement, a higher degree of skill than the old; and, unfortunately, the class of persons driven out of the old employment are not always qualified for the new one; so that a certain interval must elapse before the whole of their labour is wanted. This, for a time, produces considerable suffering amongst the working classes; and it is of great importance for their happiness that they should be aware of these effects, and be enabled to foresee them at any early period, in order to diminish, as much as possible, the injury resulting from them.

One very important inquiry which this subject presents is the question,—*Whether it is more for the interest of the working classes, that improved machinery should be so perfect as to defy the competition of hand-labour; and that they should thus be at once driven out of the trade by it; or be gradually forced to quit it by the slow and successive advances of the machine?* The suffering which arises from a quick transition is undoubtedly more intense; but it is also much less permanent than that which results from the slower process: and if the competition is perceived to be perfectly hopeless, the workman will at once set himself to learn a new department of his art. On the other hand, although new machinery causes an increased demand for skill in those who make and repair it, and in those who first superintend its use; yet there are other cases in which it enables children and inferior workmen to execute work that previously required greater skill. In such circumstances, even though the increased demand for the article, produced by its diminished price, should speedily give occupation to all who were before employed, yet the very diminution of the skill required, would open a wider field of competition amongst the working classes themselves.

That machines do not, even at their first introduction, *invariably* throw human labour out of employment, must be admitted; and it has been maintained, by persons very competent to form an opinion on the subject, that they never produce that effect. The solution of this question depends on facts, which, unfortunately, have not yet been collected . . .

Increased intelligence amongst the working classes, may enable them to foresee some of those improvements which are likely for a time to affect the value of their labour; and the assistance of Savings Banks and Friendly Societies, (the advantages of which can never be too frequently, or too strongly, pressed upon their attention,) may be of some avail in remedying the evil: but it may be useful also to suggest to them, that a diversity of employments amongst the members of one family, will tend, in some measure, to mitigate the privations which arise from fluctuation in the value of labour. Charles Babbage. *On the Economy of Machinery and Manufactures*, 4th edn, 334–7, 340–1. 1846

_____

Industrial Health Following the work of Thomas Perceval and others, several Northern doctors took up socio-medical research. Dr James Phillips Kay, later Sir J. Kay-Shuttleworth, baronet (1804–77), an Edinburgh-educated physician at Manchester, wrote movingly of the local cotton workers: 'Whilst the engine runs the people must work—men, women, and children are yoked together with iron and steam. The animal machine—breakable in the best case, subject to a thousand sources of suffering—is chained fast to the iron machine, which knows no suffering and no weariness'. Kay wrote in 1832 of overcrowded housing, a filthy atmosphere, long labour in unhealthy mills and urban immorality. In 1831 Charles Turner Thackrah (1795–1833), a Leeds surgeon, published the first edition of his celebrated book on the effects of labour on health. Trained in London, Thackrah became a well known, though often controversial, investigator, practitioner, lecturer, and author. Regularly ill himself, he devoted much of his life to searching for and condemning the causes of ill-health among the working population. The following extracts are taken from the enlarged 1832 edition of his book.

------

4   The employment of young children in any labour is wrong. The term of physical growth ought not to be a term of physical exertion. Light and varied motions should be the only effort,— motions excited by the will, not by the task-master,—the run and the leap of a buoyant and unshackled spirit. How different the scene in a manufacturing district! No man of humanity can reflect without distress on the state of thousands of children, many from six to seven years of age, roused from their beds at any early hour, hurried to the mills, and kept there, with the interval of only 40 minutes, till a late hour at night;* kept, moreover, in an atmosphere impure, not only as the air of a town, not only as defective in ventilation, but as loaded also with noxious dust. Health! cleanliness! mental improvement! How are they regarded? Recreation is out of the question. There is scarcely time

* In the Report of the Manchester Board of Health, published in 1805, the Committee remark that, "They have still to lament the untimely and protracted labour of the children employed in some of the mills, which tends to diminish future expectations, as to the general sum of life and industry, by imparing the strength, and destroying the vital stamina of the rising generation; at the same time that, in too many instances, it gives encouragement to idleness, extravagance, and profligacy in the parents, who, perverting the order of nature, subsist by the oppression of their offspring". This evil has since been remedied by a law, which applies, however, only to the cotton-mills.

for meals. The very period of sleep, so necessary for the young, is too often abridged. Nay, children are sometimes worked even in the night.

The time of labour in the flax-mills is generally excessive. When the former edition of this work was published, the people were working from half-past six in the morning till eight at night, and were allowed an interval of but 40 minutes in all that time. The engine was stopped only at noon; and the operatives consequently were obliged to take breakfast and 'drinking' while they pursued their labour,—one tending the other's machinery while the latter took his hurried meal. Children sometimes have not had the opportunity of eating till nine or ten a.m., though they had been at the mill from half-past five, and must have risen from their beds half or three-quarters of an hour before . . . Masters however enlightened and humane, are seldom aware, never fully aware, of the injury to health and life which mills occasion. Acquainted far less with physiology, than with political economy, their better feelings will be overcome by the opportunity of increasing profit, and they will reason themselves into the belief that the employment is by no means so unhealthy as some persons pretend, and that the children will be nothing the worse for two or three half-hours a-day more labour, and a little less time for meals . . . The sound of the steam-engine anticipates often, the cock-crowing of the morning. While the engine works, the people must work. Men, women, and children, are thus yoke-fellows with iron and steam; the animal machine—fragile at best, subject to a thousand sources of suffering, and doomed by nature, in its best state to a short-lived existence, changing every moment, and hastening to decay—is matched with an iron machine insensible to suffering and fatigue: all this moreover, in an atmosphere of flax-dust, for 12 or 13 hours a day, and for six days in a week . . .

COTTON-WORKERS, persons I mean who are employed in the several processes by which the plant is formed into yarn for weaving, are subjected to considerable heat, and to some injurious agencies . . .

I stood in Oxford-row, Manchester, and observed the streams of operatives as they left the mills, at 12 o'clock. The children were almost universally ill-looking, small, sickly, barefoot, and ill-clad. Many *appeared* to be no older than seven. The men, generally from 16 to 24, and none aged, were almost as pallid and thin as the children. The women were the most respectable in appearance, but I saw no fresh or fine-looking individuals among them. And in reference to all classes, I was struck with the marked contrast between this and the turn-out from a manufactory of cloth. Here was nothing like the stout fullers, the hale slubbers, the dirty but merry rosy-faced pieceners. Here I saw, or thought I saw, a degenerate race,—human beings stunted, enfeebled, and depraved,—men and women that were not to be aged,—children that were never to be healthy adults. It was a mournful spectacle. On conversing afterwards with a mill-owner, he urged the bad habits of the Manchester poor and the wretchedness of their habitations as a greater cause of debility and ill-health than confinement in factories; and from him as well as from other sources of information, it appears that the labouring classes in that place are more dissipated, worse fed, housed, and clothed, than those of the Yorkshire towns. Still, however, I feel convinced that independently of moral and domestic vices, the long confinement in mills, the want of rest, the shameful reduction of the intervals for meals, and especially the premature working of children, greatly reduce health and vigour, and account for the wretched appearance of the operatives . . . C. Turner Thackrah. *The Effects of Arts, Trades, and Professions, and of Civic States and Habits of Living, on Health and Longevity,* 2nd edn, 80–2, 144, 145–6. 1832

———

The sanitary state of urban workers had scarcely improved by the mid-nineteenth century. Cholera and other epidemics occasionally provoked fitful local agitation; Chadwick's 'Sanitary Report' of 1842 and the work of the 'Health of Towns Association' aroused some public interest; and the Public Health Act of 1848, establishing a new official Board, was a milestone in

the history of social reform. But, as Robert Baker (1803–80), a
zealous factory superintendent, showed in 1851, many workers
lived in foul conditions. A York man, Baker was a Leeds surgeon
before becoming a superintendent of factories in 1834 and an
inspector in 1858.

---

5 ... A great source of the social evils of the working classes is
their insanitary state, whether considered in a physical or a
moral point of view.

It is only just now, in the nineteenth century, that public
attention is thoroughly directed to this subject, and see! how in
many places it is received, and how persons, too obtuse to understand the great questions of life, air, ventilation, decency, and
morality, quote their fathers, as examples of longevity in the same
locations, about which such malaric mischiefs are projected,
why the theories of life and death—and of ethnological inter-
ferences should not be entertained—forgetting all the time the
difference in density of population on the same area, and with
that density, the difference in the causes of disease.

There is one thing, however, remarkable in the conduct of
most of these objectors to rational sanitary improvements, which
is, that while they endeavour to sustain this non-necessity of
intervention, they flit themselves from the paternal soil to some
more congenial site.

The great object of the builders of cottages has for many years
evidently been to plant as many dwellings upon a given area as
it would contain, without any reference whatever to health,
decency, or morality; for depend upon it, all these three essentials to human happiness are coexistent with ventilation, space,
and cleanliness. If we consider for a moment the local condition
of large manufacturing towns, we shall see how contradictory in
a sanitary point of view they are. Masses of houses have been
located in the first instance with reference to convenience of
work, crammed into the smallest possible space, divided into
streets, unpaved, unsewered, uncleansed, varying from 4 to 10
yards wide, forming squares, with sundry passages, not exceeding

3 yards wide, with here and there an unusable office—with a bad supply of water—amid the densest smoke, and by the side of pestiferous and exhalent brooks.

It may be said that these have become what they are in the course of years, that the country around them was formerly open, that the air was then less impregnated with smoke and smells, and that it is the prosperity of the place which has made them what they are.

Let all this be admitted. It is exactly a sanitary argument. Re-open them to the air and ventilation they once had—remove the nuisances which have accumulated during the course of years,— restore them to their primitive state of cleanliness! You cannot! Then convert these cottages into something else, and carry the population to other places where these essentials are to be found. Let us ask where, in such towns, do the upper classes reside? The streets in which they live are 16 or 20 yards wide. Is it for the houses or the people that this increased width is necessary? These wide streets are well sewered, paved, and flagged. Why? Because without these refinements, there could be scarcely any of the socialities of life inter-changed, and because the air from exhalent surfaces is productive of malaria. Each house has a good supply of pure water. Because water, and that ready at hand, for all purposes, is an essential element of comfort. They have large and lofty rooms, and plenty of them, because the inhabitants know how much better it is to have a good supply of pure air for health, and a division of the sexes for morality. In fact, we find everywhere there, the necessary condition of houses to health as well understood as if sanitary science had been a fundamental part of the education of their occupants. Robert Baker. *The Present Condition of the Working Classes, Generally Considered: in Two Lectures, Delivered Before the Members of the Bradford Church Institution, and Published At their Request*, 38–9. Bradford, 1851

The Factory Town   One consequence of the factory system was the rapid growth of towns, often a haphazard mixture of factories and houses. There were many complaints against the often brutal society created by such industrial growth: to Michael Sadler (1780–1835), a Leeds Tory, the factory system 'disturbed the peace of nature, making towns like to cities in a siege'. From a very different standpoint, Ernest Jones (1819–69), a well connected bourgeois Radical who became a late leader of Chartism, described both a factory town and his own lingering sentiments in poetic form. His lines were first published in the journal *The Labourer* in 1847.

6   The night had sunk along the city,
It was a bleak and cheerless hour;
The wild winds sang their solemn ditty
To cold grey wall and blackened tower.

The factories gave forth lurid fires
From pent-up hells within their breast;
E'en Etna's burning wrath expires,
But *man's* volcanoes never rest.

Women, children, men were toiling,
Locked in dungeons close and black,
Life's fast-failing thread uncoiling
Round the wheel, the *modern rack*!

E'en the very stars seemed troubled
With the mingled fume and roar;
The city like a cauldron bubbled,
With its poison boiling o'er.

For the reeking walls environ
Mingled groups of death and life:
Fellow-workmen, flesh and iron,
Side by side in deadly strife.

There, amid the wheels' dull droning
And the heavy, choking air,

Strength's repining, labour's groaning,
And the throttling of despair . . .

Stood half-naked infants shivering
With heart-frost amid the heat;
Manhood's shrunken sinews quivering
To the engine's horrid beat! . . .

Yet their lord bids proudly wander
Stranger eyes thro' factory scenes;
'Here are men, and engines yonder'.
'I see nothing but *machines*!' . . .

Thinner wanes the rural village,
Smokier lies the fallow plain—
Shrinks the cornfields' pleasant tillage,
Fades the orchard's rich domain;

And a banished population
Festers in the fetid street:—
Give us, God, to save our nation,
Less of *cotton*, more of *wheat*.

Take us back to lea and wild wood,
Back to nature and to Thee!
To the child restore his childhood—
To the man his dignity!

Ernest Jones. 'The Factory Town', in *The Battle-Day, and other poems*, 82. 1855

———

John James (1811–67), the Bradford antiquarian, first published his local history in 1840, disarming critics by writing that 'surely a book which has in most part been written after the toil of the day, and in hours stolen from recreation and sleep, is no noble game for the literary critic to pounce upon'. In the previous

c

half-century Bradford had developed rapidly, as a slow-moving backwater became a large town and the main centre of the worsted industry. In the following extract James describes the early history of the factory system in Bradford.

———

7   An enterprising gentleman, named Buckley, (residing at the time in Bradford, but who afterwards removed to Todmorden,) formed, in 1793, the design of erecting a factory here, to be wrought by a steam-engine. The land for the building had been purchased nearly opposite the Primitive Methodists' Chapel, in Manchester-road, and the respectable residents in Tyrrel-street and that quarter of the town, viewed with dread the threatened infliction of such a smoky nuisance as a steam-engine. Accordingly, a number of them signed a notice, threatening Mr. Buckley with an action at law should he persist in building the mill to be wrought by steam. This proceeding had the desired effect, as Mr. Buckley, seeing such a formidable array against him, gave up his project. As the notice has been considered in the town a curiosity, and is a great topic in any conversation relative to the introduction of factories and machinery into Bradford, I give a copy of it and a fac-simile of the names subscribed.—

>   To Mr. John Buckley, cotton-manufacturer, in Bradford, in the West-Riding of the county of York.
>   Take notice, that if either you or any person in conexion with you, shall presume to erect or build any steam-engine for the manufacture of cotton or wool, in a certain field in Horton near Bradford aforesaid, called or known by the name of the Brick-kiln Field, we whose names are hereunto subscribed shall, if the same be found a nusance, seek such redress as the law will give. Witness our hands this 23rd January, 1793.

Tom^s Atkinson	Jonas Bower
Nath:^{l} Aked	John Rand
John Smith	Wm Whitaker
Isaac Willson	Jno Hardy

Thoˢ Holdgate   Henʸ Wᵐ Oates
                       Mary Laidman
                       Betty Swaine
                       Frs. Town
                       J. Lupton
                       John Aked.

Some of the gentlemen who appended their names to this notice, were afterwards largely concerned in worsted-mills erected in the town.

Although the introduction of these mills into Bradford was thus deferred, yet the delay was only for a short time, as in 1798 Messrs. Ramsbotham, Swaine, and Murgatroyd erected one in the "Holme". The engine which supplied the propelling force was of fifteen horses' power . . .

Very soon after Ramsbotham and Swaine's mill was at work, other mills were erected in or near the town. It seems that an attempt was at that period made to introduce the cotton-manufacture here; and one mill, (at least,) which is now used in the worsted business, was, early in the present century, built for the spinning of cotton. This branch of manufactures was not, however, long carried on here.

The progress of the worsted-manufacture in Bradford, has been as rapid and as unexampled as that of its population. In 1800, according to the census, 1290 persons were employed in Bradford in trade or manufactures. In 1811, 1595 families were so employed; in 1821, 2452 families; in 1831, 3867, besides 1605 labourers. The first mill wrought by steam in Bradford, (1798), had, as before mentioned, a 15-horse engine; in 1819, the number of horses' power employed in propelling the machinery of worsted-mills in Bradford and its immediate neighbourhood, was about 492; in 1830, 1047; and now, 1840, it is upwards of 2000.

Since the year 1800, Bradford has felt fewer of the vicissitudes of trade than, it may safely be affirmed, any other trading town of its size in the kingdom. It is true its prosperity received a considerable shock by the wool-combers' strike in 1825; and the failure of Wentworth & Co.'s bank, the next year, added a more distressing blow to its trade; but, with both these drawbacks, and the mercantile embarrassments which have occurred in Bradford of late years, in common with the whole kingdom, its prosperity has been great, and almost unexampled in the history of mercantile towns, so as almost to become a proverb among its neighbours.

In and about the year 1826, power-looms were introduced into the town in considerable numbers. The riots which such introduction occasioned are before noticed. With the exception of these disturbances, Bradford has been free from the great excesses which have strongly, and for long continued periods, marked the conduct of the working classes in densely populated manufacturing districts, with respect to the use of machinery.

The ancient trade of the parish of Bradford (woollen manufacture) has almost disappeared from its tract. Its northern, eastern, and southern borders are a very correct line of demarcation between the worsted and woollen manufactures. In Eccleshill and Shipley there are two or three woollen mills, but more northernly or westernly one cannot be found in Bradford parish, nor hardly a single clothier on these quarters of or in Bradford. On the western verge of the parish a couple of cotton mills have, owing to the proximity of Lancashire, reared their heads, but they seem not to be placed in a very congenial district.

The worsted goods principally manufactured at Bradford are merinos, saxony cloths, shalloons, moreens, orleans cloths, figured crapes, and, in short, of almost every description. To an inhabitant, it is needless to mention that the whole of the wool used in these fabrics, is long wool; but to others it may be information . . .

About forty years since, Wakefield was, in these parts, the principal mart for wool; and the Bradford spinners and manufacturers, together with their neighbours, resorted to Wakefield to purchase their wool. For a considerable time past, Bradford has been the great market for wool in the north of England. John

James. *The History of Bradford and its Parish, with Additions and Continuation to the Present Time*, 273–7. 1866

The archetype of factory towns, the most discussed, praised and attacked, was Manchester, the great cotton metropolis. 'The awakening of a Manchester, on Monday morning, at half-past five by the clock; the rushing off of its thousand mills, like the boom of an Atlantic tide, ten thousand times ten thousand spools and spindles all set humming there—it is perhaps, if thou knew it well, sublime as a Niagara, or more so,' wrote Carlyle. Other observers found this rapidly growing corner of Sir Oswald Mosley's estates depressing and unpleasant. The liberal William Cooke Taylor (1800–49) here describes the virtues and defects of an expanding town, already attracting immigrant labour, in a letter to his friend Richard Whateley (1787–1863), Archbishop of Dublin.

8 ... I shall proceed to examine the social condition of Manchester which may be considered as the metropolis of the cotton manufacture. No person, however casual a visitor, can for a moment mistake the character of the town. It is essentially a place of business, where pleasure is unknown as a pursuit, and amusements scarcely rank as secondary considerations. Every person who passes you in the street has the look of thought and the step of haste. Few private carriages are to be seen; there is only one street of handsome shops, and that is of modern date; there are some very stately public buildings, but only one of them is dedicated to recreation, the rest are devoted to religion, charity, science, or business ... The men are as businesslike as the place, and in their character a zeal for religion, charity, and science is not less conspicuous than the buildings consecrated to these objects are in the town. I might adduce as proofs the subscriptions to the fund for building churches, to the Methodist Centenary Fund, to the funds for relieving the citizens of Hamburgh, for erecting the Lancashire Independent College, for supporting the numerous literary and scientific institutions in the town and its neighbourhood; nor will gratitude permit me to omit the hospitable and magnificent reception given to the members of the British Association at its late meeting in Manchester, though the visit was paid at a season of general depression and great commercial distress.

Were I asked how a stranger could best form a notion of the character of the Manchester manufacturers, I should recommend him to visit the Exchange of Manchester at the period of "high change"; that is, about noon on a Tuesday. It is the parliament of the lords of cotton—their legislative assembly—which enacts laws as immutable as those of the Medes and Persians, but, unlike every other parliament in the world, very much is done and very little is said. Nowhere can there be found so practical a comment on the well-known line,—

Silence that speaks, and eloquence of eyes.

Transactions of immense extent are conducted by nods, winks, shrugs, or brief phrases, compared to which the laconisms of the ancient Spartans were specimens of tediousness and verbosity. There is a kind of vague tradition, or rather remote recollection, that a man was once seen to gossip on the Exchange: it was mentioned in the terms one would use if he saw a saraband danced in St. Peter's, or Harlequin playing his antics at the Old Bailey. For my own part, I felt my loquacious tendencies so chilled by the genius of the place, that I deemed myself qualified to become a candidate for La Trappe.

The characteristic feature of the assembly is talent and intelligence in high working order; genius and stupidity appear to be equally absent; but if the average of intellect be not very high, it is evident that not a particle of it remains unemployed. It has been my fortune to visit this place in a season of great commercial prosperity and activity, and more recently at this period of stagnation and depression. On the first occasion, a stranger would imagine that he had got into one of those communities of dancing dervishes whose rule inculcates silence and perpetual motion. It seemed as if each man was incapable of remaining in the same spot for three continuous seconds: it is the principle of a Manchester man that "nought is done where aught remains to do:" let him have but the opportunity, and he will undertake to supply all the markets between Lima and Pekin, and he will be exceedingly vexed if, by any oversight, he has omitted a petty village which could purchase a yard of cloth or a hank of yarn. The marks of Manchester manufacturers are as well known in Bokhara or Samarcand as in Liverpool or London, and its patterns guide taste equally under the burning sun of Africa and amid the snows of Siberia.

The aspect of the Exchange at this period of commercial distress is perfectly appalling: there is a settled gloom on every countenance, accompanied with a restlessness of eye quite out of keeping with the contracted brow and the compressed lip. Eagerness is changed into obstinacy; men seem to feel that their profits, if not their capitals, are slipping from their hands, and they have made up their minds to bear a certain amount of loss, but not to endure one fraction more . . .

I have been thus particular in describing the symptoms of commercial prosperity or commercial distress on the Exchange of Manchester, for I know of no other part of the town in which you can easily obtain certain indications of either the one or the other. Contrary to general belief, experience has shown me that Manchester does not afford a fair specimen of the factory population in any of the conditions of its existence, and that the outward aspect of the place affords a very imperfect test of the state of the trade in South Lancashire. It must, in the first place, be observed that there is always, and must necessarily be, considerable distress in a place where there is a large demand for untrained labour. Though the factories require skilled labour, yet there are many occupations connected with the commerce of cotton which only demand the exertion of brute strength; such, for instance, are porterage, lighterage, coal-heaving, &c. This demand for untrained labour is not so great as in Liverpool, nor could Manchester exhibit anything so low in the social scale as the dock-population of that port; still the demand exists to a considerable

extent, and is mainly, if not entirely, supplied by immigrants
from Ireland, Wales, Scotland, and the English agricultural
counties. In consequence of the rapidity of the growth of manufactures in Manchester, the increase of population very rapidly
outstripped the means of accommodation; even the factory
operatives are badly lodged, and the dwellings of the class below
them are the most wretched that can be conceived. This is particularly the case in the township of Manchester: its narrow
streets, its courts and cellars, have been abandoned to the poorest
grade of all. There they live, hidden from the view of the higher
ranks by piles of stores, mills, warehouses, and manufacturing
establishments, less known to their wealthy neighbours,—who
reside chiefly in the open spaces of Cheetham, Broughton, and
Chorlton,—than the inhabitants of New Zealand or Kamts-
chatka.

Your Grace is aware that to some extent Dublin is similarly
divided into the city of the rich and the city of the poor; but I
know that many respectable and wealthy manufacturers reside
in the liberties of Dublin, while the smoke-nuisance drives everybody from the township of Manchester who can possibly find
means of renting a house elsewhere. These conditions necessarily
produce an unhealthy condition of society, both physically and
morally. I find that in the township of Manchester the rate of
mortality is so high as 1 in 30; and, making every allowance for
the swelling of the number of deaths by aged and sickly immigra-
tion from the rural districts, this rate indicates a very large
amount of misery and suffering arising from causes purely
physical.

Another evil of fearful magnitude arises from this separation of
Manchester into districts in which relative poverty and wealth
form the demarkation of the frontiers. The rich lose sight of the
poor, or only recognise them when attention is forced to their
existence by their appearance as vagrants, mendicants, or delin-
quents. It is a very common error to attribute to the factories the
evils which really arise from an immigrating and non-factory
population; a population, too, which has been recently increased

by the great demand for unskilled labour produced by the works and excavations required for the new railways which are radiating on every side from Manchester. I took some pains to ascertain the character of this immigrating population, and I found it such as to account, in a very great degree, for the high rate of mortality and the low condition of morals in the township of Manchester. It appeared that peasants inadequate to the fatigues of rural toil frequently come into the towns with the hope of finding some light employment suited to their feeble strength, and that persons whose character is blighted in the country seek to escape notice in the crowd of the town. Having conversed with many of these persons, and also made inquiries from the guardians of the poor and the administrators of public charities, I am persuaded that Manchester must long continue to present an appearance of great destitution and delinquency which does not belong to the town itself, but arises from a class of immigrants and passengers. W. Cooke Taylor. *Notes of a Tour in the Manufacturing Districts of Lancashire; in a Series of Letters to His Grace the Archbishop of Dublin,* 2nd edn, 9–15. 1842

While some writers were dismayed by the gloomy social conditions of the factory towns, others found the energy and organisation of the new industries exhilarating and admirable. Even the 'Young England' Tories were divided; while the novelist Disraeli noted the dreariness and lack of amenities his friend George Smythe, 7th Viscount Strangford (1818–57), saw Manchester as a modern Venice. In the following lines John Jones, an operative spinner at McConnell & Kennedy's Manchester mills, expresses one worker's local patriotism—contriving at the same time to praise his employers.

9   Now see the Cotton from the town convey'd
       To Manchester, that glorious mart of trade:
       Hail splendid scene! the Nurse of every art,
       That glads the widow's and the orphan's heart!

Thy mills, like gorgeous palaces, arise,
And lift their useful turrets to the skies!
See Kennedy's stupendous structure join'd
To thine M'Connell—friends of human kind!
Whose ready doors for ever wide expand
To give employment to a numerous band,
Murray's behold! that well deserves a name,—
And Lee's and Houldsworth's our attention claim,—
And numerous others, scattered up and down,
The sole supporters of this ample town.
        John Jones. *The Cotton Mill.* Manchester, 1821

The 'social novel' supplemented the social reports of commissioners and journalists during the 1840s. A good example was
the second 'Young England' volume of Benjamin Disraeli
(1804–81), later Conservative prime minister and earl of
Beaconsfield. Disraeli was concerned both to reconcile the 'two
nations' of rich and poor and to romanticise the notion of a
feudal aristocracy. His style combined a sometimes florid senti-
mentality with perceptive observation. In the following extract
Disraeli portrays a handloom weaver and his home. The picture
is probably based on conditions observed while visiting his
friend W. B. Ferrand at Bingley in 1844; certainly, some of the
scenery described in the novel was taken from Ferrand's rugged
estate.

---

10 It was a single chamber of which he was the tenant. In the
centre, placed so as to gain the best light which the gloomy
situation could afford, was a loom. In two corners of the room
were mattresses placed on the floor, a check curtain, hung upon
a string if necessary, concealing them. In one was his sick wife;
in the other, three young children: two girls, the eldest about
eight years of age; between them their baby brother. An iron
kettle was by the hearth, and on the mantelpiece, some candles,
a few lucifer matches, two tin mugs, a paper of salt, and an iron
spoon. In a farther part, close to the wall, was a heavy table or

dresser; this was a fixture, as well as the form which was fastened by it.

The man seated himself at his loom; he commenced his daily task.

"Twelve hours of daily labour, at the rate of one penny each hour: and even this labour is mortgaged! How is this to end? Is it rather not ended?' And he looked around him at his chamber without resources: no food, no fuel, no furniture, and four human beings dependent on him, and lying in their wretched beds, because they had no clothes. 'I cannot sell my loom', he continued, 'at the price of old firewood, and it cost me gold. It is not vice that has brought me to this, nor indolence, nor imprudence. I was born to labour, and I was ready to labour. I loved my loom, and my loom loved me. It gave me a cottage in my native village, surrounded by a garden, of whose claims on my solicitude it was not jealous. There was time for both. It gave me for a wife the maiden that I had ever loved; and it gathered my children round my hearth with plenteousness and peace. I was content: I sought no other lot. It is not adversity that makes me look back upon the past with tenderness.

"Then why am I here? Why am I, and six hundred thousand subjects of the Queen, honest, loyal, and industrious, why are we, after manfully struggling for years, and each year sinking lower in the scale, why are we driven from our innocent and happy homes, our country cottages that we loved, first to bide in close towns without comforts, and gradually to crouch into cellars, or find a squalid lair like this, without even the common necessaries of existence; first the ordinary conveniences of life, then raiment, and, at length, food, vanishing from us.

"It is that the capitalist has found a slave that has supplanted the labour and ingenuity of man. Once he was an artisan: at the best, he now only watches machines; and even that occupation slips from his grasp, to the woman and the child. The capitalist flourishes, he amasses immense wealth; we sink, lower and lower; lower than the beasts of burden; for they are fed better than we are, cared for more. And it is just, for according to the present system they are more precious. And yet they tell us that the interests of Capital and Labour are identical." Benjamin Disraeli. *Sybil, or The Two Nations*, Book II, ch 13. 1845

Factory Life Much literature appeared in the 1830s purporting to describe the lives of factory workers. In 1832 John Brown issued his horrifying *Memoir of Robert Blinco*, a child apprentice in the Derbyshire cotton mills; and in 1841 William Dodd, 'the Factory Cripple', published a *Narrative of* [his] *Experiences and Sufferings*—a terrible recital of overwork and ill-treatment on which considerable doubts were later cast. Much of this popular literature was published as sentimental poetry. The following lines by Michael Sadler, 'The Factory Girl's Last Day', are typical of many publications.

11

'Twas on a winter's morning,
  The weather wet and wild,
Three hours before the dawning
  The father roused his child;
Her daily morsel bringing,
  The darksome room he paced,
And cried, 'The bell is ringing,
  My hapless darling, haste!'

'Father, I'm up, but weary,
  I scarce can reach the door,
And long the way and dreary,—
  O carry me once more!
To help us we've no mother;
  And you have no employ;
They killed my little brother,—
  Like him I'll work and die!'

Her wasted form seemed nothing,—
  The load was at his heart;
The sufferer he kept soothing
  Till at the mill they part.

The overlooker met her,
  As to her frame she crept,
And with his thong he beat her,
  And cursed her as she wept.

Alas! What hours of horror
  Made up her last day;
In toil, and pain, and sorrow,
  They slowly passed away:
It seemed, as she grew weaker,
  The threads they oftener broke,
The rapid wheels ran quicker,
  And heavier fell the stroke.

The sun had long descended,
  But night brought no repose;
Her day began and ended
  As cruel tyrants chose.
At length a little neighbour
  Her halfpenny she paid,
To take her last hour's labour,
  While by her frame she laid.

At last, the engine ceasing,
  The captives homeward rushed;
She thought her strength increasing—
  'Twas hope her spirits flushed:
She left, but oft she tarried;
  She fell and rose no more,
Till, by her comrades carried,
  She reached her father's door.

All night, with tortured feeling,
  He watched his speechless child;
While, close behind her kneeling,
  She knew him not, nor smiled.

Again the factory's ringing
  Her last perceptions tried;
When, from her straw-bed springing,
  ' 'Tis time!' she shrieked, and died!

That night a chariot passed her,
  While on the ground she lay;
The daughers of her master
  An evening visit pay:
Their tender hearts were sighing,
  As negro wrongs were told,
While the white slave lay dying
  Who gained their father's gold!
    Michael Sadler. 'The Factory Girl's Last
      Day'. 1832

The Dawsholm Printfield (or Printworks) was established in Maryhill, Glasgow in 1750 by a local merchant, William Stirling, as a linen printing establishment. After many changes of fortune (which greatly affected the local population) the business became a major institution in the burgh (which was annexed by Glasgow in 1891). The local historian here recalls some aspects of working-class life in the early nineteenth century.

12 During the time George Yuille, Shortridge & Co. carried on Dawsholm Printfield, and also after the firm was changed to Daniel Gilchrist & Co., a store was carried on inside the work until the passing of the Truck Act. Everything in the shape of clothing, food, and drink was sold to the workers. The rules and customs in printworks at that time were of the most oppressive and tyrannical kind, and had a most demoralizing tendency. The principle branches of calico printing were—1st, pattern designing, putting-on, sketchmaking; 2nd, print-cutting; 3rd, engraving; 4th, block-printing; and 5th, machine printing, confined principally to flat press printing, there being then little cylinder printing. A young man apprenticed to any of these

branches had to pay a sum of money to the members of the particular branch of the business he intended learning in the work. This was technically called an entry. Seven and ten guineas were usually exacted, and in my father's case, who began his apprenticeship in Dawsholm as a pattern designer early in 1818, my grandfather had to pay some thirteen guineas. These heavy exactions so crippled families, hanging like a millstone about their necks, that it was sometimes years before they could get their heads above water. Had this money been put to any good or useful purpose, such as a sick fund, or to meet the entry of orphans into these trades, or any others, or a sum of money been given to the widows of members at death, there might have been some excuse for the uncompromising manner compliance with these payments was so rigidly insisted on; but it was mostly always spent in a guzzle with lots of drink, setting some of the more thirsty and thoughtless members on the spree (or the fuddle as it was generally called) for a day or two and even longer.

At that time all the apprentices were regularly indentured (my late father's indentures is now in my possession). I have heard him frequently tell how on one occasion a number of young apprentices had been entered to the block-printing, and there were nearly £80 to be spent. It all went in drink, some of the printers carrying home their share of whiskey, rum, &c., in stoups and cans. This style of things was simply disgraceful. Here were clear cases of 'man's inhumanity to man'. But the exactions did not stop with the paying of the entry-money; there were continual demands made for additional fees and all for one object—to be consumed in drink. If a block-printer, he had to pay a pint of whiskey when he printed his first handkerchief and grounded it; another for his first garment pieces; another for his first furniture piece; for his first shave; for his first long-tailed coat; and other reasons which must be nameless, and to think these demands were made by men (some of them married and even elderly men) on young lads was shocking in the extreme. But the worst of the matter was that the drinking of these pints, as they were called, was frequently carried on in the workshop. Here was an example and training that one can only characterise as most deplorable . . . Alexander Thomson. *Random Notes and Rambling Recollections of . . . Maryhill, 1750–1894,* 16–17. Glasgow, 1895

———

The ancient burgh of Dundee was for centuries a considerable textile centre in north-eastern Scotland. The local trade with the Baltic encouraged the development of the linen industry— which, from the 1830s, gradually yielded to the manufacture of jute. Primarily reliant on its staple industry and far from other industrial communities, nineteenth-century Dundee was dominated by a tightly connected oligarchy of Liberal capitalists. Eventually headed by the Baxter family, the flax and jute 'barons' provided little for Dundee beyond low-paid employment for workers from the burgh, the immediate hinterland, and Ireland; but they created long lasting bitterness. Dundee's vile conditions provoked protests from doctors, Presbyterian and Episcopalian clergymen, and a remarkable group of working-class Radical writers. A celebrated publication of the proletarian 'Dundee Republic of Letters' was contributed anonymously (but apparently by one Frank Forrest, son of an Australian convict) to the *Northern Warder* newspaper. It was reissued in book form by James Myles (1819–51), mason, Chartist, bookseller, author, and publisher, in 1850. Authorship was subsequently ascribed to Myles, and it is probable that he at least edited the work. The moving story of a country boy driven to mill-work is here recorded at some length.

———

13 To begin at the beginning, I may succinctly state that my father was a country shoemaker, and, like most of his class, somewhat speculative; fond of political and religious disputation, and not altogether devoid of a taste for 'the bottle'. In addition to carrying on a trade in the locality, which, by the way, was in the vicinity of Glammis, he likewise rented a small "pendicle" of about six acres . . . Can the reader blame me then, when I affirm that I think the little cottage where I was born was the sweetest spot on earth. The tidy garden, the river, the thick plantations, over which towered the grey turrets of the ancient castle of Glammis, the soothing solace of an affectionate mother's love, and all the innocent amusements and prattling of youth's warm existence, rush on my memory, and force me to conclude that I have seen no place like the place of my childhood. The dim remembrances that I yet have of these happy days impress me with the belief that my father and mother lived comfortably, and knew nothing of want and its grim attendants; but alas, evil days were in store for us, and the erring footsteps of a parent brought misery on himself, an innocent wife, and helpless family —so true is it that the sins of the father are visited upon the children. Let me briefly detail the catastrophe alluded to.

. . . One year my father attended [Glamis] market for the purpose of selling a young cow which he had fed for the butchers. After disposing of the animal, he entered a tent with a few friends, and indulged somewhat freely in whisky potations. He was naturally quiet and obliging in his everyday demeanour, but when unhinged by the whisky demon, he was contradictory and quarrelsome in his disposition, so much so that my mother, who on usual occasions wielded a great influence over his mind, wept with very fear when she saw him coming home intoxicated. On the evening in question, he sat long and drank deeply, and while doing so a person belonging to the parish of Kettle, who at one time was guilty of a highly dishonourable action towards him, entered the tent. Both were the worse for drink. Old sores were harshly touched. High words passed, and from words they came to blows, and, alas, my father struck him a dreadful blow on the head with a heavy staff, which felled him to the ground in a state of utter insensibility, and after lingering nearly six hours in unconscious existence he breathed his last . . . A few months of weariness and grief rolled by, and my father was brought up for trial at the High Court of Justiciary, Perth. He at once pled guilty to culpable homicide, and the public prosecutor accepted the plea. A numerous and respectable array of testimonials and

D

witnesses to character were produced in court, but the judge dwelt severely on the fact that there was ill-will existing in my father's mind against the deceased at the time the unhappy event occurred; and as intoxication could not, under any circumstances, be admitted as an extenuation for crime, considering his duty to society he could not, he said, sentence him to less punishment than seven years' transportation . . . When my mother received the intelligence of his sentence, she felt a sorrowful gratitude, as she fearfully anticipated a more terrible doom, and with a fervent faith that all was for good, she gradually resigned herself to her lot. After my father's conviction she was obliged to sell her cow, to defray some legal expenses incurred, and at the following term, the laird, in conjunction with a few unbending creditors, rouped the whole of her little stock and household furniture, excepting a chest of drawers she had got as a dowry from her father and some other trifles. She was thus left almost destitute, and the crime of my father having raised an ignorant prejudice against her, she determined on leaving the place which had witnessed the disgrace of her husband and the social degradation of herself and two children. From the general wreck of her worldly fortunes she managed to save a few blankets and sheets, a bedstead, and the chest of drawers spoken of. Though a severe trial to her, she was obliged to sell the latter to a neighbour for £2. 10/-. She then packed up her little property and consigned it to the carrier who in those days traded between Dundee and Glammis, and with a heavy heart left the spot rendered sacred to her by many endearing associations, and retired to hide her poverty in the busy regions of a great manufacturing town. It was on a warm morning in May, when I had scarcely reached my seventh year, that we set out on foot. I asked my mother if we were going to see my father. She gave me no direct answer, but told me we were going where I would see many strange sights, and where I would require to work in a spinning mill, to help to keep her living. My young heart bounded with pleasure at the prospect of seeing Dundee, a town that I had heard the country people speak of as very large; and by their conversations I had concluded that there was no place equal to it ...

Those who have spent all their days in the country feel awkward, and even lonely, when they first settle in a large town ... My new home was indeed a great change for a romping country boy, such as I then was. I had been accustomed to live in the fresh air of creation, to sport by the river that rolled past our secluded cot, to gaze on the green fields and rustling trees which beautified Strathmore, and to listen to the bleating of sheep, the lowing of cows, or the caroling of the skylark, warbling his matins at the portals of heaven; but now I was shut up in a narrow close where nothing could be seen but old dirty walls of stone and lime; and the music of the morning which fell on my ear was not the sweet songs of birds, but the harsh guttural roars of coal sellers and fish cadgers.

... My mother now laid down what she conceived a workable programme for our future guidance. She purchased a pirn wheel, and secured the winding of pirns for two handloom weavers. She then applied at several spinning mills for work to me, but did not succeed. This dampened her hopes considerably, and, on the evening of her unsuccessful search, she sat down exhausted, and wept bitterly. To see a strong man "begging a brother of the earth to give him leave to toil", willing to work, unable to want, yet cannot get labour, is, says an eminent writer, "a melancholy sight", but methinks a mother forced to make her child a slave, depending for bread on the use of its bones and sinews, willing to sacifice these, offering them in the market, and unable to command a purchaser, is a more dismal picture still, and drives the contemplative mind to question the Christianity of civilization, where such pictures can be seen. Our support now depended on my mother's own energies, and, though she rose every morning by five o'clock, and toiled on until nine and ten at night, she could not earn above 6d. and 7d. per day, or on an average 3s. 3d. per week. Those accustomed to such labour will make a little more, but it being new to my mother, she could only gain this pittance by fifteen or sixteen hours close application. Every Monday morning she had to pay 11d. for rent, which left her with about 2s. 4d. for our support. On this small sum, and a few shillings that remained of the money which she received for her drawers, we lived four weeks. On the beginning of the fifth week, I got work in a spinning mill at the Dens, which filled our hearts with joy, but so near starvation were we then, that my mother had only 4½d. in the world. It was on a Tuesday morning in the month of "Lady June" that I first entered a spinning mill. The whole circumstances were strange to me. The dust, the din, the work, the hissing and roaring of one person to another, the obscene language uttered, even by the youngest, and the imperious commands harshly given by those "dressed in a little brief authority", struck my young country heart with awe and astonishment. At that time the twelve hours' factory act had not come into operation, and spinning mills were in their glory as huge instruments of demoralization and slavery. Mercenary manufacturers, to enable them to beat more upright employers in the markets, kept their machinery and hands active fifteen, and, in many cases, seventeen hours a-day, and, when tender children fell asleep under prolonged infliction of 'work! work! work!', overseers roused them with the rod, or thongs of thick leather burned at the points. The lash of the slave driver was never more unsparingly used in Carolina on the unfortunate slaves than the canes and "whangs" of mill foremen were then used on helpless factory boys. When I went to a spinning mill I was about seven years of age. I had to get out of bed every morning at five o'clock, commence work at half-past five, drop at nine for breakfast, begin again at half-past nine, work until two, which was the dinner hour, start again at half-past two, and continue until half-past seven at night. Such were the nominal hours; but in reality there were no regular hours, masters and managers did with us as they liked. The clocks at the factories were often put forward in the morning and back at night, and instead of being instruments for the measurement of time, they were used as *cloaks* for cheatery and oppression. Though this was known amongst the hands, all were afraid to speak, and a workman then was afraid to carry a watch, as it was no uncommon event to dismiss anyone who presumed to know too much about the science of horology. In country mills, a more horrific despotism reigned than in Dundee. There, masters frequently bound the young by a regular contract which gave them a more complete control over their labour and liberties than taking them from week to week. In one establishment in the vicinity of Dundee, the proprietor, a coarse-minded man, who by accident had vaulted out of his natural element into the position of a "vulgar rich" man, practised the contract system, and had bothies where he lodged all his male and female workers. They were allowed to cook, sleep, and live in any dog and cat manner they pleased, no moral superintendence whatever being exercised over them. His mill was kept going 17 and frequently 19 hours per day. To accomplish this all meal hours were almost dispensed with, and women were employed to boil potatoes and carry them in baskets to the different flats; and the children had to swallow a potato hastily in the interval of putting up "ends". On dinners cooked and eaten as I have described, they had to subsist till half-past nine, and frequently ten at night. When they returned to their bothies, brose, as it is a dish that can be quickly made, constituted their suppers, for they had no time to wait the preparation of a different meal. They then tumbled into bed: but balmy sleep had scarcely closed their urchin eyelids, and steeped their infant souls in blessed forgetfulness, when the thumping of the watchmen's staff on the door would rouse them from repose, and the words, "Get up; it's four o'clock", reminded them they were factory children, the unprotected victims of monotonous slavery. At this mill, and indeed all mills, boys and girls were often found sleeping in stairs and private places, and they have been seen walking about the flats in a deep sleep, with cans of "sliver" in their hands. When found in this state, they were caned or kicked according to the mood of their superiors. One poor boy, who is still alive, and who, by force of mind, great persistency and rectitude, rose to be a mercantile clerk in Dundee, and now fills a responsible situation on one of the principal

railways in England, was for some time in this factory. One day
he was carrying an armful of bobbins from one flat to another.
When ascending the stair, he sat down to rest, as his legs were
sore and swollen by incessant standing. In a few moments he
was fast asleep. Whilst enjoying this stolen repose, the master
happened to pass. Without the least warning he gave him a
violent slap on the side of the head, which stunned and stupified
him. In a half-sleeping state of stupefaction he ran to the roving
frame, which he sometimes attended, and five minutes had
barely elapsed when his left hand got entangled with the
machinery, and two of his fingers were crushed to a jelly, and
had to be immediately amputated. His unfeeling taskmaster
gave him no recompense—in fact never asked after him; he was
left to starve or die, as Providence might direct. The reader will
no doubt imagine that boys working 18 and 19 hours a-day
would have nearly double wages to boys at the present time, who
only work ten. I can only speak from experience, and what has
come under the range of my own knowledge on this point. When
I went to the mill, I was paid with 1s. 6d. per week, and my
nominal hours, as already remarked, were 13 hours per day.
When the Twelve Hours' Act was in operation, boys had from 3s.
up to 4s. per week; and now since the Ten Hours' Act came into
force, their wages vary from 3s. 3d. to 4s. 3d. In short, as far as I
can learn, their wages are as good under the Ten Hours' Act as
they were under the Twelve Hours' Act. Of course the Act precludes such young boys as I was from working; yet, considering
the hours I was confined and the wages I was paid with, the
contrast is highly favourable to the humanity and wisdom of
those good men who procured protection to factory children,
and said to competition and capital, "Hitherto shalt thou come
but no further".

My first day's experience as a factory boy damped my ardour,
and, on returning home to my mother, I cried bitterly. In the
flat in which I was employed there were seventeen girls from
nine to twenty-five years of age, and I was the only boy. When
the mill was set on, I experienced the most indescribable sensa-

tion. I looked strange and even stupid, and when I glanced to any of my companions, as if supplicating sympathy; they returned my kindness by making wry faces and gestures, in ridicule of my country appearance. At the meal hours the other boys of the work gathered round me, as if I had been a natural curiosity imported from some distant clime. They "streaked my buttons", swore, and challenged me to fight; and soon I found I would get no peace to live unless I risked the contingency of a battle. As there is honour among thieves, so I found a modicum of honour amongst mill boys, as one about my own age was selected to be my adversary. Accordingly we adjourned to a park near the Dens, and had a regular "mill", and in the crowd were animals called men prompting us on. It so happened that I proved the best pugilist, and ever afterwards I got more peace to attend my work, go and return from my meals, as I then was looked on as a member of the fraternity. About a week after I became a mill boy, I was seized with a strong, heavy sickness, that few escape on first becoming factory workers. The cause of this sickness, which is known by the name of the "mill fever", is the pestiferous atmosphere produced by so many breathing in a confined place, together with the heat and exhalations of grease and oil. All these causes are aggravated in the winter time by the immense destruction of pure air by the gas that is needed to light the establishment. This fever does not often lay the patient up. It is slow, dull, and painfully wearisome in its operation. It produces a sallow and debilitated look, destroys rosy cheeks, and unless the constitution be very strong, leaves its pale impress for life. I have already mentioned the wages paid to boys under the Twelve and Ten Hours' Act, and the wages I received myself when there was no act. I may likewise refer to the wages of the female spinners. Those who were employed at the mill I first entered, received fully higher remuneration than what is now paid to the same class; but the reduction cannot by any show of facts or reason be ascribed to factory legislation. In 1824 the spinning trade was very brisk in this locality, and female spinners received 10s. per week, for which they attended 36 to 40 spindles during 15 or 16 hours every lawful day. At present a female spinner will attend from 100 to 120 spindles, according to the character of the material, and her wages range from 5s. 9d. to 6s. per week. Though she manages nearly double the quantity of spindles at present as compared with 1824, yet this does not result from extra labour being imposed on her, but from the extensive improvements in machinery since that date. It will thus be seen by the above comparison, which is as unfavourable a one as I could draw for the short-time system, inasmuch as it places in juxtaposition an extra brisk time with the present, which is only moderate, that the wages of female labour is fully 40 per cent less than in 1824; but the simple cause of this is keener competition in that department of the labour market, which has been greatly aggravated by the immense influx of Irish women during the last twenty years; and though no factory act had been conceived or carried into execution, similar effects would have flowed from the causes indicated.

If further evidence was needed to demonstrate the justice and correctness of this conclusion, it may be found in the fact, that the wages of spinners in 1832 before factory legislation extended to Dundee, and, when they worked thirteen hours a day, were 6s. and 6s. 6d. per week, being only a mere fraction more than what they now receive under the beneficent reign of the Ten Hours' Bill. [James Myles]. *Chapters in the Life of a Dundee Factory Boy*, 2–15. Dundee, 1850

Visits to the Factories   During the early nineteenth century it became increasingly obligatory for visitors to the industrial areas to examine local industries. Foreign royalty was conducted around selected showplaces, while British and Continental tourists roamed virtually at will. Some were delighted and fascinated by novel industrial organisation; some were horrified by what they saw. John Arthur Roebuck (1802–79), a Radical MP who opposed factory reform, was dismayed by a Glasgow cotton factory in 1837: 'The heat was excessive . . . the stink pestiferous . . . I nearly fainted!' Louis Simond (1767–1831), a

French-born American subject, had visited the Scottish cotton districts earlier. In the following extracts he describes mills at New Lanark and Glasgow.

14 Returning to Lanark, we stopped a moment at a cotton-manufactory. It was the first established in Scotland, and the most considerable. It is certainly a prodigious establishment. We saw four stone buildings, 150 feet front each, four stories high of twenty windows, and several other buildings, less considerable; —2500 workmen, mostly children, who work from six o'clock in the morning till seven o'clock in the evening, having in that interval an hour and a quarter allowed for their meals; at night, from eight to ten for school. These children are taken into employment at eight years old, receiving five shillings a-week; when older, they get as much as half-a-guinea. Part of them inhabit houses close to the manufactory, others at Lanark, one mile distance; and we were assured the latter are distinguished from the others by healthier looks, due to the exercise this distance obliges them to take,—four miles a-day. Eleven hours of confinement and labour, with the schooling, thirteen hours, is undoubtedly too much for children. I think the laws should interfere between avarice and nature. I must acknowledge, at the same time, that the little creatures we saw did not look ill.

The prodigious increase of manufactories in England, and the application of the force of water to their machinery, threatened equally the purity of mountain-streams and of morals; but farther improvements in mechanics have led to another mode of applying the force of water, and, instead of its weight, its expansion is now made subservient to the arts. The steam-engine is an agent so convenient, so powerful, and so economical, in a country abounding with fossil coal, that falls of water have been abandoned; but the great manufactory of Lanark had been established before this great discovery. The cost of the steam-engine and fuel is more than compensated by the advantage of saving the transportation of both the rough materials and the manufactured articles; of being on the spot of consumption and exportation, and where great population furnishes workmen, rather than among deserts and mountains. I understand that there are now even grist-mills worked by the steam-engine . . .

. . . On our arrival at Glasgow this morning [24 August, 1810] . . . Professor M., Mr. G. and Mr. H. . . . undertook to carry us immediately to the principal manufactories. We have seen carding and spinning-mills, weaving-mills, mills for everything. The human hand and human intelligence are not separated; and mere physical force is drawn from air and water alone, by means of the steam-engine.*Manufactories, thus associated with science, seem to produce with the facility and fecundity of nature. It is impossible to see without astonishment these endless flakes of cotton, as light as snow, and as white, ever pouring from the carding-machine, then seized by the teeth of innumerable wheels and cylinders, and stretched into threads, flowing like a rapid stream, and lost in the *tourbillon* of spindles. The eye of a child or of a woman, watches over the blind mechanism, directing the motions of her whirling battalion, rallying disordered and broken threads, and repairing unforeseen accidents. The shuttle likewise, untouched, shoots to and fro by an invisible force; and the weaver, no longer cramped upon his uneasy seat, but merely overlooking his self moving looms, produces forty-eight yards of cloth in a day, instead of four or five yards.

Passing rapidly from one thing to another, you have only time

*A steam-engine, of the power of forty horses, consumes about five chaldrons, or 11,000lbs. weight of coals in twenty-four hours; and notwithstanding the great cheapness of coals, the keeping of 120 horses (three sets of 40, to relieve each other), would not cost more than double the price of the fuel; therefore, in a country where fuel costs more than double the price here, the steam-engine could not be used to advantage. This great consumption of fuel, by confining the steam-engine to a coal country, secures, in a great degree, to England, to the exclusive privilege of a prodigious power, alone sufficient to give her a decided superiority in the practice of most of the useful arts. It is more than a century since the principles of the steam-engine were discovered, and applied to mechanical uses, but it is not more than twenty-five or thirty years since this machine, I might almost say this living body, was brought to its present state of perfection, by the celebrated Mr. Watt. . . .

to wonder, without understanding enough to explain satisfactorily what you have seen, or scarcely to retain any connected remembrance of it. One thing, however, made an impression, from its ingenious futility,—the tambouring or embroidering *mill*. Multitudes of needles, self-moving, execute, as by enchantment, a regular pattern of sprigs or flowers. This machine has the appearance of the stocking-loom. I do not know whether there is not a dying mill; the force of water is used at least in the process, to press the yarn after it has been dipped, and to squeeze out the dye . . .

Many of these manufactories requiring an even temperature of about 70°, which exceeds that of the external air, the windows are kept constantly shut; indeed they are often constructed so as not to open at all, or at most only one pane in a window, and the atmosphere is, as may be supposed, not very pure. Some of the processes require even 90° or 100°, obtained by means of large fires in stoves, winter and summer. We just looked in, and the heat appeared quite insupportable to us, although we have often experienced it for days together in America. The men did not seem to suffer from it; the external air was today 55° to 60°. [Louis Simond]. *Journal of a Tour and Residence in Great Britain, during the years 1810 and 1811, by a French Traveller: with Remarks on The Country, Its Arts, Literature, and Politics, and on the Manners and Customs of its Inhabitants*, I, 278–9, 283–6. Edinburgh, 1815

Mrs Frances ('Fanny') Trollope (1780–1863), the mother of the novelist Anthony and herself a popular writer, turned her attention to factory conditions in 1839. Armed with Lord Ashley's introductions to Northern reformers, she and her eldest son, Thomas Adolphus (1810–92), toured Yorkshire and Lancashire in February and March. They were dismayed by 'horrors of uncivilised savagery and hopeless abject misery', and Frances soon published a novel in twelve parts. Thomas later insisted that 'there was no exaggeration . . . What we are there described to have seen, we saw'. However, Mrs Trollope incorporated information dating from various periods. Her villain, the cotton

master Sir Matthew Dowling, expresses exaggerated Anti-Corn
Law League views; his horrific friend Elgood Sharpton is
apparently based on Ellice Needham of Litton; Messrs Wood
and Walker are praised by name; Parson Bull of Bierley becomes 'Parson Bell of Fairley'. The novel is interesting partly as
an early form of sentimental propaganda and partly because it
was based upon research in the factory districts.

---

15 The party entered the building, whence—as all know who
have done the like—every sight, every sound, every scent that
kind nature has fitted to the organs of her children, so as to
render the mere unfettered use of them a delight, are banished
for ever and for ever. The ceaseless whirring of a million hissing
wheels, seizes on the tortured ear; and while threatening to
destroy the delicate sense, seems bent on proving first, with a
sort of mocking mercy, of how much suffering it can be the
cause. The scents that reek around, from oil, tainted water, and
human filth, with that last worst nausea, arising from the hot
refuse of atmospheric air, left by some hundred pairs of labouring
lungs, render the act of breathing a process of difficulty, disgust,
and pain. All this is terrible. But what the eye brings home to the
heart of those, who look round upon the horrid earthly hell, is
enough to make it all forgotten; for who can think of villainous
smells, or heed the suffering of the ear-racking sounds, while they
look upon hundreds of helpless children, divested of every trace
of health, of joyousness, and even of youth! Assuredly there is no
exaggeration in this; for except only in their diminutive size,
these suffering infants have no trace of it. Lean and distorted
limbs—sallow and sunken cheeks—dim hollow eyes, that speak
unrest and most unnatural carefulness, give to each tiny,
trembling, unelastic form, a look of hideous premature old
age.

But in the room they entered, the dirty, ragged, miserable
crew, were all in active performance of their various tasks; the
overlookers, strap in hand, on the alert; the whirling spindles
urging the little slaves who waited on them, to movements as

unceasing as their own; and the whole monstrous chamber, redolent of all the various impurities that "by the perfection of our manufacturing system", are converted into "gales of Araby" for the rich, after passing in the shape of certain poison, through the lungs of the poor . . .

The moment at which Michael Armstrong entered the cotton mill at Deep Valley, was a critical one. The summer had been more than commonly sultry, and a large order had kept all hands very sharply at work. Even at dead of night the machinery was never stopped, and when one set of fainting children were dragged from the mules another set were dragged from the reeking beds they were about to occupy, in order to take their places. The ventilation throughout the whole fabric was exceedingly imperfect; the heat, particularly in the room immediately beneath the roof, frightfully intense; cleanliness as to the beds, the floors, and the walls, utterly neglected; and even the persons of the children permitted to be filthy to excess, from having no soap allowed to assist their ablutions—though from the greasy nature of their employment it was peculiarly required, while the coarse meal occasionally given out to supply its place was invariably swallowed, being far too precious in the eyes of the hungry children to be applied to the purpose for which it was designed. In addition to all this, the food was miserably scanty, and of a nature so totally unfit to sustain the strength of growing children thus severely worked, that within a fortnight after Michael's arrival, an epidemic fever of a very alarming description began to shew itself. But it had made considerable progress, before the presence of this new horror was revealed to him. Frances Trollope. *The Life and Adventures of Michael Armstrong, The Factory Boy*, 79–80, 212. 1840

———

William Cooke Taylor, a prolific writer on the factory industries, staunchly supported the proprietors against their detractors. In the following extract he paints a sympathetic and idealised picture of the Turton mills under the rule of the Liberal Quaker brothers Edmund (1801–81) and Henry Ashworth (1794–1880).

Keen supporters of the Anti-Corn Law League and the New
Poor Law, the Ashworths were also among the most bitter and
extreme opponents of workers' unions and factory reform.
Popular contemporary literature inevitably showed less respect
to Quaker employers, such as the Ashworths and John Bright
(1811–89) of Rochdale, who were strongly against reform, than
has been customary recently.

16   The Oaks, Turton, near Bolton.

How a painter would have enjoyed the sight which broke upon
my waking eyes this morning! To my right is one of the tribu-
taries to the Irwell, winding through the depths of a richly
wooded and precipitous valley, or rather ravine; the sun's rays,
glinting from the waters, come like flashes through every opening
in the foliage, warning me that I have remained a laggard without being able to plead fatigue as an excuse,—it being now a
settled maxim that nobody is to be tired from a journey by railway. Before me, at the extreme of the level on which I stand . . .
is the Hall in the Wood, memorable for having been the residence
of Crompton . . . Beyond is the hill on which a great part of the
busy town of Bolton is built. The intervening valley is studded
with factories and bleach-works. Thank God, smoke is rising
from the lofty chimneys of most of them! for I have not travelled
thus far without learning, by many a painful illustration, that the
absence of smoke from the factory-chimney indicates the quench-
ing of the fire on many a domestic hearth, want of employment
to many a willing labourer, and want of bread to many an honest
family. The smoke too creates no nuisance here—the chimneys
are too far apart; and it produces variations in the atmosphere
and sky which, to me at least, have a pleasing and picturesque
effect.

From this description every man in Lancashire will see that I
am an inmate of the house of Mr. Henry Ashworth, and will
pardon me for resolving not to say one syllable respecting him or
his family. Were I to attempt to speak of them as they deserve,
those who know them would exclaim that I had done injustice to

their merits, and those who do not know them would accuse me of flattery . . .

The Turton Mill is built in the bottom of the ravine, just under the owner's residence, from which, however, it is separated by the little stream I have already noticed. It is a plain stone building, but not without some pretensions to architectural beauty. On descending to visit it, my attention was excited at the entrance by a very simple circumstance, which I think not unworthy of record. Fruit-trees, unprotected by fence, railing, or palisade, are trained against the main wall of the building, and in the season the ripe fruit hangs temptingly within reach of every operative who goes in or out of the mill. There is not an instance of even a cherry having been plucked, though the young piecers and cleaners must pass them five or six times every day . . .

The interior of Mr. Ashworth's mill does not differ materially from that of many other well-regulated mills which I have visited, such as Ashton's of Hyde, Taylor's of Preston, and a host of others. I was, however, pleased to find that great care had been bestowed upon the "boxing up" of dangerous machinery. I learned that accidents were very rare, and that, when they did occur, they were, as my own senses convinced me that they must have been, the result of the grossest negligence or of absolute wilfulness. I mention this circumstance because the burst of sentimental sympathy for the condition of the factory-operatives which, a few years ago, frightened the isle from its propriety, appealed largely to the number of accidents which happened from machinery, and I was myself for a time fool enough to believe that mills were places in which young children were, by some inexplicable process, ground—bones, flesh, and blood together—into yarn and printed calicoes. I remember very well when first I visited a cotton-mill feeling something like disappointment at not discovering the hoppers into which the infants were thrown. I have since found that such absurdity is only credited by those who, like myself at that period, could not tell the difference between a cotton-mill and a tread-mill. But a very little consideration should have taught me better: derange-

ments of machinery are very expensive accidents to remedy; and
if the mill-owners of Lancashire were as reckless of human life as
the worst of their assailants have chosen to describe them, they
certainly are not men likely to disregard their own pockets. I
have had some opportunities of estimating the cost of accidents,
and I know that the engineer's bill is considerably heavier than
the surgeon's. Without at all giving millowners credit for more
than the average philanthropy of their countrymen, I am quite
ready to repose confidence in their anxiety to prevent accidents,
because their own obvious interests are a tolerably safe security
for their humanity.

The conditions of health in the mills of Turton and Egerton,
and I may add generally in all that I have examined, are exceedingly favourable. The working rooms are lofty, spacious,
and well ventilated, kept at an equable temperature, and
scrupulously clean. There is nothing in sight, sound, or smell to
offend the most fastidious sense. So much space is occupied by
the machinery that crowding is physically impossible. I should
be very well contented to have as large a proportion of room and
air in my own study as a cotton-spinner in any of the mills of
Lancashire. With respect to the length of time during which the
work is continued, I must remark that the toil is not very great,
nor is it incessant. The heaviest part of the labour is executed by
the steam-engine or the water-wheel; and there are so many
intervals of rest, that I am under the mark when I assert that an
operative in a cotton-factory is at rest one minute out of every
three during the period of his nominal employment. On the
other hand, these intervals of rest are brief and quick in their
recurrence; they cannot therefore be turned to any useful
account. Hence I should not be indisposed to give favourable
consideration to a time-bill, if its advocates could show me how
the time of labour could be shortened without the amount of
wages being reduced. Some of them no doubt will say, compel
the employers to pay still the same amount of wages, because in
all ages of the world that philanthrophy has been fashionable
which consists in being exceedingly generous at the expense of

other people; but I should like to know by what process employers could be forced to pay a rate of wages disproportionate
to their profits . . . W. Cooke Taylor. *Notes of a Tour in the Manufacturing Districts of Lancashire* . . . , 2nd edn, 21–7. 1842

PART TWO

Factory Reform

The factory system did not inaugurate long hours, child labour, low wages, and bad working conditions. But when it added to these traditional aspects of life managerial control, urban congestion, regular speeding-up of machinery, the new social and economic philosophies, and a widening 'class' difference between owners and workers it provoked attack. Medical and humanitarian influence lay behind the first Sir Robert Peel's 'Health and Morals of Apprentices Act' of 1802. By this measure the so-called apprentices, virtually given to rural millowners by the Poor Law authorities, were restricted to 12 hours' daily labour, with no night work. The growing use of steam-power permitted the cotton industry to move into towns, where local children could be employed without restriction. Consequently, from 1815 Robert Owen proposed further legislation, and Peel took up the cause, demanding that children aged 10–18 should be restricted to 10½ hours labour, plus 1½ hours for meals and 30 minutes for education. A Commons Committee in 1816 and two Lords Committees (under the sympathetic Lord Kenyon, an Evangelical Tory) in 1818 and 1819 heard evidence; but Peel's Act of 1819 merely restricted children aged 9–16 to 12 hours' labour, plus 1½ hours for meals, in the cotton mills. A considerable agitation, led by northern Anglican priests, doctors, some merchants, and several workers, had been raised, backed by the Manchester merchant Nathaniel Gould. But the demand for reform was dangerous: workers who gave evidence were often dismissed and blacklisted. The Whig-Radical J. C. Hobhouse proposed an 11-hours Bill for children in 1825, but succeeded only in restricting night work; and in 1829 a further Act slightly improved this measure. By 1830 legislation ostensibly limited children in cotton mills to 12 hours' actual work, leaving other child-workers 'free'. The Factory Movement, largely Tory in leadership and Anglican in religious inspiration, started a humanitarian crusade against such a situation. While it campaigned on behalf of the wretched factory children, the Movement always hoped for a general reduction of working hours, and its eventual success marked a major breach in governmental *laisser-faire* attitudes.

Child Labour It is often forgotten that child labour existed long before the development of the factory. Not only was it economically essential to the domestic system of production but it was also widely admired by such observers as John Wesley (1703–91) for teaching the virtues of labour and discipline and preventing youthful vice. In the following extract Samuel Crompton's eldest son George recalls his work at the age of 4.

17 I recollect that soon after I was able to walk I was employed in the cotton manufacture. My mother used to bat the cotton wool on a wire riddle. It was then put into a deep brown mug with a strong ley of soap suds. My mother then tucked up my petticoats about my waist, and put me into the tub to tread upon the cotton at the bottom. When a second riddleful was batted I was lifted out, it was placed in the mug, and I again trode it down. This process was continued until the mug became so full that I could no longer safely stand in it, when a chair was placed besides it, and I held on by the back. When the mug was quite full, the soap suds were poured off, and each separate *dollop* of wool well squeezed to free it from moisture. They were then placed on the bread-rack under the beams of the kitchen-loft to dry. My mother and my grand-mother carded the cotton wool by hand, taking one of the *dollops* at a time, on the simple handcards. When carded they were put aside in separate parcels ready for spinning. Gilbert J. French. *The*

Life and Times of Samuel Crompton, 3rd edn, 58–9. Manchester, 1862

Sir Robert Peel's Committee of 1816 heard a variety of conflicting evidence on industrial conditions, and as a result Parliament did not legislate for three more years. The following extracts illustrate the Committee's difficulties. The first section is taken from the examination of James Pattison, a director of the East India Company and a silk manufacturer at Congleton in Cheshire. He employed some 310–30 workers. The total included twelve aged 6–7, twenty-three aged 7–8 and nineteen aged 8–9, earning between 1s 6d and 4s weekly; and 129 aged 10–18 earning between 3s and 8s 6d. The 114 or 115 adults earned 9s–15s for men and 4s 6d–9s for women. About thirty workers were 'aged' (50–80 years old). The children worked 12½ hours daily, including 2 hours for meals. The second extract is from the evidence of Theodore Price, a Warwickshire JP.

---

18   What is the state of health of the children and persons employed in your manufactory?—I may say, from my own experience of nearly forty years, unexceptionally good; there has never been a contagious disorder in the mill since I have known it, and there has been none in the town since the year 1754 ...

Could the children be conveniently taught within the mills daily?—That is a point which, not having tried it, it might be difficult for me to answer; but as I understand it has been tried in other mills, I may venture to say, that from what I have learned of the practice of those other mills, it would be productive of very great inconvenience.

Could any system of inspection of the mills be established without inconvenience?—I conceive certainly not; some years ago it was very much the practice for persons to visit mills of this description from curiosity, but it was found so inconvenient, that those visits have been declined as much as possible, as the attention of the children was always drawn from their duty by the appearance of any new faces; and inspectors, for the purpose of seeing all is right, it is conceived by those who are the best judges of the question, would very much weaken the authority of the masters over the children. . . .

Why do you take the children so young?—The motive of taking the children so young is partly to oblige their parents; in a great degree to relieve the township; and also, because at that early age their fingers are more supple, and they are more easily led into the habit of performing the duties of their situation. . . .

Are the Committee to understand, that children of six or seven years of age are employed ten hours and a half?–Yes.

Have you ever observed any inconvenience to the health of those very young children from being employed so many hours? —I can only state . . . that they enjoy very excellent health . . .

Do you not conceive, that a regulation preventing children of six, seven or eight years of age from working more than eight hours a day, would ultimately increase their strength and promote their growth?—If I had been in the habit of indulging myself in abstract matters, I might be able to answer the question; but my answer goes only to practical experience of what is the effect; the comparative state of health they would enjoy in another situation, is an abstract question which I am not competent to answer.

You have never found that the children of six, seven or eight years of age, from being worked ten hours and a half, have sallow countenances, or inclination to the rickets, or any of those effects which arise from children at an early period of life being overworked?—I do not reside on the spot myself, but I pay occasional visits, and have always been very much satisfied with the state of health of the children I have employed . . .

Do you conceive that working in the factories is favourable to the morals of young people?—So far favourable to it, if I may venture to say so, that it keeps them out of mischief; and while they are industriously employed, they are less likely to contract evil habits than if they are idling their time away.

*　　　*　　　*

What is your opinion of the employment for girls in cotton mills, of a certain age?—I should think it cruel in the extreme to oblige females, under certain circumstances, to be walking for ten or twelve hours a day.

Have you been frequently called upon as a magistrate, to sign indentures for parish apprentices?—Yes, parish apprentices' indentures have been signed by me a great many years ago, but latterly, for mills, not any.

... From the observations you made at this mill [at Emscot, near Warwick], would you as a magistrate, be inclined to give your consent to the apprenticeship of children to those mills?— I never will sign an indenture to a cotton mill so long as I live, that is, under the present existing laws.

What was the general impression made upon your mind, with respect to the employment of children in this mill?—Very bad; the impression was unfavourable. I have four daughters, and I say upon my word of honour, that if I was put to the choice either to send them to this cotton mill for seven years, or to Warwick Bridewell, I would prefer the latter.

Have you had any experience of the condition of cotton mills, but the one to which you have alluded?—I saw no other. Report of Minutes of Evidence respecting the state of health and morals of children employed in Manufactories; chiefly as to cotton factories, *Parliamentary Papers*, 1816, III, 76–9, 122

————

The best known, though controversial, account of children's work in the factories was the Report of Michael Sadler's Select Committee of 1832. It has often been attacked on the grounds that the evidence sometimes referred to earlier periods, but contemporary opponents never convincingly refuted it. Eighty-seven witnesses contributed to the 682-page Report, but the last unreformed Parliament was dissolved before publication, and the masters' evidence had not been heard. Furthermore, Sadler was defeated at the Leeds election in December 1832, and so the work had to be started again. The following extracts are taken from the evidence of three Yorkshire witnesses, Abraham Whitehead, a Scholes clothier; Abraham Wildman (1803–70), a Radical poet, tradesman, and secretary of the Keighley Short Time Committee; and Samuel Coulson, a Stanningley tailor. They represent three typical viewpoints.

------

19 ... I have seen children during this last winter coming from work on cold dark nights between 10 and 11 o'clock, although trade has been so bad with some of the mills that they have had nothing to do; others have been working seventeen or seventeen and a half hours per day ... I can tell you what a neighbour told me six weeks ago; she is the wife of Jonas Barrowcliffe, near Scholes; her child works at a mill nearly two miles from home, and I have seen that child coming from its work this winter between 10 and 11 in the evening; and the mother told me that one morning this winter the child had been up by two o'clock in the morning, when it had only arrived from work at eleven; it had then to go nearly two miles to the mill, where it had to stay at the door till the overlooker came to open it ... They had no clock; and she believed, from what she afterwards learnt from the neighbours, that it was only 2 o'clock when the child was called up and went to work; but this has only generally happened when it has been moonlight, thinking the morning was approaching.

The general cry in the West Riding of Yorkshire is, that there is too much produced; that there is over-production; and they think that if the markets became drained of the goods, and if the demand be increased, the price of goods produced will advance likewise; when the markets are full of goods, the prices will generally sink; and when the prices are low, the wages fall too. Now by a strict and proper regard to time, we think there will be an advance in goods.

At what time in the morning, in the brisk time, did those girls go to the mills?—In the brisk time, for about six weeks, they have gone at 3 o'clock in the morning, and ended at 10, or nearly half-past, at night.

What sort of mills were those?—The worsted mills.

What intervals were allowed for rest or refreshment during those nineteen hours of labour?—Breakfast a quarter of an hour, and dinner half an hour, and drinking a quarter of an hour . . .

What was the length of time they could be in bed during those long hours?—It was near 11 o'clock before we could get them into bed after getting a little victuals, and then at morning my mistress used to stop up all night, for fear that we could not get them ready for the time; sometimes we have gone to bed, and one of us generally awoke.

What time did you get them up in the morning?—In general me or my mistress got up at 2 o'clock to dress them.

So that they had not above four hours' sleep at this time?— No, they had not.

For how long together was it?—About six weeks it held; it was only done when the throng was very much on; it was not often that.

The common hours of labour were from 6 in the morning till half-past 8 at night?—Yes.

With the same intervals for food?—Yes, just the same.

Were the children excessively fatigued by this labour?— Many times; we have cried often when we have given them the little victualling we had to give them; we had to shake them, and they have fallen to sleep with the victuals in their mouths many a time.

Had any of them any accident in consequence of this labour? —Yes, my eldest daughter when she went first there . . .

Did this excessive term of labour occasion much cruelty also? —Yes, with being so very much fatigued the strap was very frequently used . . .

What was the wages in the short hours?—Three shillings a week each.

When they wrought those very long hours what did they get? —Three shillings and sevenpence halfpenny . . .

. . . they were expected to lay out part of their wages under the truck system?—Yes.

Report from the Select Committee on the 'Bill to regulate the Labour of Children in the Mills and Factories of the United Kingdom', *Parliamentary Papers*, 1831–2, XV, 19, 156, 192–3.

The Leadership of Richard Oastler Richard Oastler (1789–1861) was the real founder of the Factory Movement. Reared as a Methodist, he became a staunch member of the Church of England and 'a Church and King Tory'. After failing as a small Leeds merchant, he inherited his father's post as steward to the Thornhill family's estate at Fixby Hall near Huddersfield. A discussion with John Wood of Bradford convinced him of the need to reform Yorkshire industry. His clarion call in the Liberal *Leeds Mercury* instantly provoked controversy in the autumn of 1830 and was followed by a succession of widely read letters. By 1831 Oastler was organising campaigns for Hobhouse's Bill and forging a Tory-Radical alliance which was to have considerable effects on Northern politics. He became an effective writer and rousing speaker, which made him the idolised 'Factory King' of the textile areas.

---

20   YORKSHIRE SLAVERY
To the Editors of the Leeds Mercury
'It is the pride of Britain that a slave cannot exist on her soil; and if I read the genius of her constitution aright, I find that slavery is most abhorrent to it—that the air which Britons breathe is free—the ground on which they tread is sacred to liberty'. *Rev. R. W. Hamilton's Speech at the Meeting held in the Cloth-hall Yard, September 22d*, 1830.

Gentlemen,—No heart responded with truer accents to the sounds of liberty which were heard in the Leeds Cloth-hall Yard, on the 22d instant, than did mine, and from none could more sincere and earnest prayers arise to the throne of Heaven, that hereafter slavery might only be known to Britain in the pages of her history. One shade alone obscured my pleasure, arising not from any difference in principle, but from the want of application of the general principle *to the whole empire*. The pious and able champions of *negro* liberty and *colonial* rights should, if I mistake not, have gone farther than they did; or perhaps, to speak more correctly, before they had travelled so far as the West Indies, should, at least for a few moments, have sojourned in our own immediate neighbourhood, and have directed the attention of the meeting to scenes of misery, acts of oppression, and victims of slavery, even on the threshold of our homes.

Let truth speak out, appalling as the statement may appear. The fact is true. Thousands of our fellow-creatures and fellow-subjects, both male and female, the miserable inhabitants of a *Yorkshire town*, (Yorkshire now represented in Parliament by the giant of anti-slavery principles) are this very moment existing in a state of slavery, *more horrid* than are the victims of that hellish system '*colonial slavery*'. These innocent creatures drawl out, un-pitied, their short but miserable existence, in a place famed for its profession of religious zeal, whose inhabitants are ever fore-most in *professing* 'temperance' and 'reformation', and are striv-ing to outrun their neighbours in missionary exertions, and would fain send the Bible to the farthest corner of the globe—aye, in the very place where the anti-slavery fever rages most furiously, her *apparent charity* is not more admired on earth, than her *real cruelty* is abhorred in Heaven. The very streets which re-ceive the droppings of an 'Anti-Slavery Society' are every morn-ing wet by the tears of innocent victims at the accursed shrine of avarice, who are *compelled* (not by the cart-whip of the negro slave-driver) but by the dread of the equally appalling thong or strap of the over-looker, to hasten, half-dressed, *but not half-fed*, to those magazines of British infantile slavery—*the worsted mills in the town and neighbourhood of Bradford*! ! !

Would that I had Brougham's eloquence, that I might rouse the hearts of the nation, and make every Briton swear, 'These innocents shall be free!'

Thousands of little children, both male and female, *but princi-pally female*, from seven to fourteen years of age, are daily *compelled* to *labour* from six o'clock in the morning to seven in the evening, with only—Britons, blush while you read it!—*with only thirty*

minutes allowed for eating and recreation. Poor infants! ye are indeed sacrificed at the shrine of avarice, *without even the solace of
the negro slave*; ye are no more than he is, *free agents*; ye are compelled to work as long as the *necessity* of your needy parents may
require, or the cold-blooded avarice of your worse than bar-
barian masters *may demand*! Ye live in the boasted land of freedom, and *feel* and mourn that *ye are slaves*, and slaves without the
only comfort which the negro has. He knows it is his sordid,
mercenary master's interest that he should *live*, be *strong* and
healthy. Not so with you. Ye are doomed to labour from morning
to night for one who cares not how soon your weak and tender
frames are stretched to breaking! You are not mercifully valued
at so much per head; this would assure you at least (even with
the worst and most cruel masters) of the mercy shown to their
own labouring beasts. No, no! your soft and delicate limbs are
tired and fagged, and jaded, at only *so much per week*, and when
your joints can act no longer, your emaciated frames are cast
aside, the boards on which you lately toiled and wasted life
away, are instantly supplied with other victims, who in this
boasted land of liberty are HIRED—not sold—as slaves and daily
forced to hear that they are free. Oh! Duncombe! Thou hatest
slavery—I know thou dost resolve that 'Yorkshire children shall
no more be slaves!' And Morpeth! who justly glorieth in the
Christian faith—Oh, Morpeth! listen to the cries and count the
tears of these poor babes, and let St. Stephen's hear thee swear
'they shall no longer groan in slavery!' And Bethell, too! who
swears eternal hatred to the name of slave, whene'er thy manly
voice is heard in Britain's senate, assert the rights and liberty of
Yorkshire youths. And Brougham! thou who art the chosen
champion of liberty in every clime! oh bend thy giant's mind,
and listen to the sorrowing accents of these poor Yorkshire little
ones, and note their tears; then let thy voice rehearse their woes,
and touch the chord thou only holdest—the chord that sounds
above the silvery notes in praise of heavenly liberty, and down
descending at thy will, groans in the horrid caverns of the deep
in muttering sounds of misery accursed to hellish bondage; and

as thou sound'st these notes, let Yorkshire hear thee swear, 'Her
children shall be free!' Yes, all ye four protectors of our rights,
chosen by freemen to destroy oppression's rod,

> 'Vow one by one, vow altogether, vow
> With heart and voice, eternal enmity
> Against oppression by your brethren's hands;
> Till man nor woman under Britain's laws,
> Nor son nor daughter born within her empire,
> Shall buy, or sell, or HIRE, or BE A SLAVE!'

The nation is now most resolutely determined that negroes
shall be free. Let them, however, not forget that Britons have
common rights with Afric's sons.

The blacks may be fairly compared to beasts of burden, *kept for
their master's use*; the whites, to those *which others keep and let for hire*.
If I have succeeded in calling the attention of your readers to
the horrid and abominable system on which the worsted mills in
and near Bradford is conducted, I have done some good. Why
should not children working in them be protected by legislative
enactments, as well as those who work in cotton mills? Christians
should feel and act for those whom Christ so eminently loved,
and declared that 'of such is the Kingdom of Heaven'.—I
remain, yours, etc.,

A Briton.

Fixby Hall, near Huddersfield, Sept. 29, 1830.

Leeds Mercury, 16 October 1830

21   SLAVERY IN YORKSHIRE

TO THE WORKING CLASSES OF THE WEST RIDING OF THE COUNTY OF
YORK

My Friends,—Sir J. C. Hobhouse's bill for shortening the hours
of labour in ALL factories is lost! Yes, the bill, on which you had
fixed your fondest hopes, is vanished! Aye, my friends, that bill
which had enlivened the hearts of your poor Factory children,
which had for once implanted the gleam of hope in *their* hearts,
and taught *them* to chaunt in songs of praise the name of Hob-

house—is abandoned by its author! Your hopes—your infants'
hopes, are suddenly blighted! . . . Bend not, however, to despair
—but trust in God, and in yourselves—the God of justice,
of mercy, and of truth, still reigns—and he will plead your
cause . . .

After all, we are told that we live in the land of liberty; and if
we attempt to rescue British infants from slavery, we are, forsooth, the friends of the slave trade, and are only raising the hue
and cry to turn the attention of the nation from West Indian
slavery. Yes, my fellow-countrymen, this has been said a thousand times since the factory system was exposed. The real friends
of tyranny have put on the mask of philanthropy, and, with the
cry of 'no slavery', would rivet the chains upon *your* children, all
the time persuading you they are the only 'Liberals' of the day.
From such turn away! And be ye assured that no man, be his
pretensions what they may, can really wish to emancipate the
poor black slave in the West Indies, who refuses his aid and
assistance in emancipating *your* children from a state of slavery
more horrid than that by which the infants of the slaves in the
West Indies are cursed. Be duped no longer! Willingly lend your
assistance to emancipate black slaves; but *imperatively* require
from those members of parliament, ministers of religion and its
professors, as well as the *'factory masters'* who solicit your aid in
favour of the blacks, that they shall prove their sincerity, and
that they really do hate slavery, by encouraging and signing
petitions in favour of 'ten hours a day' as the limit of your children's work . . .

. . . For the future your path is plain. Let no promises of support from any quarter sink you to inactivity. *Consider that you must
manage this cause yourselves*, nor think a single step is taken so long
as any constitutional effort is left untried. Establish, instantly
establish, committees in every manufacturing town and village,
to collect information *and publish facts*. The public, generally, do
not know what it is; then tell them how it has gone on destroying
the health and morals of the people; how it operates in families
by preventing the growth of those parental and filial affections

which nature has implanted in every breast, but which this hateful system habitually eradicates. Show also how the baneful effects of the destruction of these feelings, afterwards, operate on society! Tell, how the factory system beggars the industrious domestic manufacturer! *Count, if you can, the hundreds of respectable families who have been driven from comfort and independence by the all-powerful operation of this monopolising system*! Point to the poor rates, and show how it has filled the ranks of the paupers; and never forget that these 'liberal factory masters' are not quite so 'liberal' as the tyrannical slave-holder! . . .

. . . Yes, yes! bring all these facts before the public, and show the hideous monster in his native glare. Then ask, shall he go on conquering and to conquer, *until the manufacture of the empire is concentrated under one large roof, and the world is supplied by one gigantic firm*? Till human nature is almost physically and morally destroyed, *and all the inhabitants of this land shall be the slaves of one great manufacturing nabob*. Let your committees call on every Christian, and particularly on every Christian minister, and respectively solicit their aid. Surely no follower of Christ can withhold his assistance. In due time call public meetings, and there plead the cause of the poor infant sufferers, and expose the horrors of the factory system; then prepare petitions to parliament, praying it to interfere in the sacred cause of suffering humanity; and, on every election for members of parliament, use your influence throughout the empire to prevent any man being returned who will not *distinctly and unequivocally pledge himself to support a 'Ten Hours a day and a Time-book Bill'*. If you will instantly begin to work on this plan, and *steadily pursue it*, you are sure of success. It is impossible that a system so cruel, so injurious, so unjust, so unchristian, can stand in a Christian country when once the eyes of the public are open to its horrors. *Your present failure points the road to your certain success*! . . .

. . . Let your politics be 'TEN HOURS A DAY, AND A TIME-BOOK'; and whoever offers himself as a candidate at any future election, unless he will *solemnly pledge* himself to these two points, REFUSE HIM YOUR SUPPORT! Don't be deceived: you will hear the cries of

—'No slavery'—'Reform'—'Liberal principles'—'No monopoly', &c. But let your cries be—'No Yorkshire slavery'—'No
slavery in any part of the empire'—'No factorymongers'—'No
factory monopolists'. If you are determined, rest assured you will
succeed. Your children will be liberated from a bondage greater
than they would have inherited had they been born of negro
slaves. Once more—be not led astray by the perpetual cry of
'liberal principles'. Depend upon it, the man who will refuse to
'liberate' your children is neither 'liberal' nor a 'hater of slavery'.
Now then, my friends, for 'a long pull, a strong pull, and a pull
altogether!' Victory is yours, if you are true to yourselves! *Let
the tyrants know that you have sworn,* 'OUR CHILDREN SHALL BE FREE!'
—I am, my friends, a sincere enemy to slavery in every form, in
every part of the world, and your sincere well-wisher,

RICHARD OASTLER

Fixby Hall, near Huddersfield, Oct. 10th, 1831.

Leeds Intelligencer, 20, *Leeds Patriot,* 22 October 1831

22 One Sunday morning, when we were all preparing to go to
church, about half-a-dozen working men, from Huddersfield,
called upon me. They had read my letters in the newspapers
about 'Yorkshire slavery'; they informed me that they wished to
converse with me about those letters of mine, and that they came
on behalf of the factory-workers of Huddersfield, to thank me for
them, and to offer their best assistance to me. I told them that 'I
was going to church, and that on any other day I should be glad
to see them'. They replied, 'Sunday, Sir, is the only day on which
we can come; we are in the mills all the rest of the week, from
early in the morning till late at night'. This information brought
home most forcibly to my mind, that the factory system and the
fourth commandment could not work together. I thought the
matter over, consulted with Mrs. Oastler, and, seeing that it was
clearly a work of charity, remained with them; the rest of the
family went to church. Those men being factory-workers, gave
me much useful information, invited me to communicate freely

with them, and offered, cordially, to co-operate with me, in
striving to obtain a change in the factory system. I heard all they
had to say with great interest. I was struck with their intelligence
and their civility. I had seen much of the poor when in sickness
and distress at their homes, and in the workhouse and infirmary,
but till that day I had never entered into communion with
working men on matters related to themselves as a class connected with their employers. A new field seemed open to me.
Those men surprised me by the knowledge which they com-
municated and the sensible manner in which they conveyed that
knowledge to me. Still I thought there were hindrances to our
working together, I being a tory and a churchman, they radicals
and dissenters; therefore, after thanking them, I said, 'It will be
better that we work separately, you taking your course, I taking
mine.' They thought differently. After a good deal of conversation we agreed to work together, with the understanding, that
parties in politics, and sects in religion, should not be allowed to
interfere between us. That agreement has never been broken.
The Home, 6 March 1852

Though often assailed as a Chartist, a Radical, and an incen-
diary, Oastler remained a Tory Churchman. He justified his
bitter hostility to long industrial hours and the bleak New Poor
Law of 1834 by reference to Evangelical belief and a romantic
hierarchic High Toryism. His increasingly violent career was cut
short in 1840, when he was imprisoned in the Fleet Prison as a
debtor to his employer, Thomas Thornhill. From his cell, he
produced a weekly journal, *The Fleet Papers*, in which he continued his campaign. The following extract explains his philosophy.

23 A Tory is one who, believing that the institutions of this
country are calculated, as they were intended, to secure the
prosperity and happiness of every class of society, wishes to
maintain them in their original beauty, simplicity, and integrity.
He is tenacious of the rights of all, but most of the poor and needy,

because they require the shelter of the constitution and the laws more than the other classes. A Tory is a staunch friend of Order, for the sake of Liberty; and, knowing that all our institutions are founded upon Christianity, he is, of course, a Christian; believing with St. Paul, that each order of society is mutually dependent on others for peace and prosperity, and that, although "there are many members, yet there is but one body . . ." Sir, I am just such a Tory; or, if you prefer it in my own words, as I once defined it to the Duke of Wellington, when he asked me, "What do you mean by Toryism?" You shall have it:—I replied "My Lord Duke, I mean a place for everything, and everything in its place". "A good day's wages for a fair day's work." "The King, happy, secure, and venerated in his palace,—the nobles, happy, secure, and honoured in their castles,—the bankers, merchants, and manufacturers, happy, secure, and beloved in their mansions,— the small tradesmen and shopkeepers happy, secure and respected in their homes, and the labourers happy, secure, and as much respected as the best of them, in their cottages. And I mean also that they should all be enabled, humbly, reverently, and nationally to worship the God of their fathers. This is what I mean by Toryism, my Lord Duke". The Duke smiled, and expressed himself as being much pleased with my definition of Toryism. If I am mistaken in the name, I know that I am not in my creed. I fear that the noble Duke has forgotten the Tory creed . . .

If you prefer a more concise definition of my Toryism, you have it in the toast, which I first gave at the dinner table of my friend, the friend of his country and her institutions, the late Michael Thomas Sadler, (and which I have often seen on our banners since)—"The Altar, The Throne, and The Cottage". I shall never forget the pleasure which poor Sadler evinced, when I first gave that toast . . .

I never changed my name—I never saw any charm in the word "Conservative". I am still an old-fashioned ultra-Tory, who firmly believes, that the farther we wander from our sound constitutional and Christian institutions into the labyrinth of ex-

F

pediency, the nearer we approach to anarchy or despotism. *The Fleet Papers*, I, 5, 30 January 1841

The Factory Reformers   The men who rallied behind Oastler were a very varied group, predominantly Tory or Radical in politics and Anglican or Primitive Methodist in religion. From 1831 they formed a network of Short Time Committees throughout the textile districts, to organise demonstrations, propaganda, and petitions. An early disciple and thenceforth a lifelong friend of Oastler was a young Yorkshire squire, William Busfeild Ferrand (1809–89), a Bingley landowner, sportsman, determined Protectionist, and the unruly Tory MP for Knaresborough in 1841–7. His blistering attacks on industrialists earned him the title of 'the Working Man's Friend'. In Oastler's journal *The Home* he recalled his 'conversion'.

24   It was soon after Sadler and Oastler unfurled the banner of protection that I became a public man. At the hour of five on a winter's morning, I left my home to shoot wild fowl. On my road, I had to pass along a deep and narrow lane which led from a rural village to a distant factory. The wind howled furiously— the snow fell heavily, and drifted before the bitter blast. I indistinctly traced three children's footsteps. Soon, I heard a piteous cry of distress. Hurrying on, again I listened, but all was silent except the distant tolling of the factory bell. Again I tracked their footmarks, and saw that one had lagged behind; I returned, and found the little factory slave half-buried in a snow-drift fast asleep. I dragged it from its winding sheet; the icy hand of death had congealed its blood and paralysed its limbs. In a few minutes it would have been "where the wicked cease from troubling and the weary are at rest". I aroused it from its stupor and saved its life. From that hour I became a "Ten Hours' Bill Man" and the unflinching advocate of "protection to native industry!" W. B. Ferrand. "Letters to the Duke of Newcastle"—I, 8 January 1852, in *The Home*, 27 March 1852

Thomas Pitt (1792–1858), a Lancashire workman, represented a 'moderate' section in the agitation, and sometimes opposed Yorkshire militancy. He supported the well meaning but generally ineffective Radical manufacturer MPs Joseph Brotherton (1783–1857) and Charles Hindley (1800–57). But he played a full rôle in the agitation, devoting much of his life to meetings, rallies, and canvassing.

---

25 The late Mr. Pitt was born at Astley, in Lancashire, and was brought up to hand-loom weaving. When about 31 years of age he came to reside at Newton Moor, and obtained employment at Ashton's cotton mills, as a cotton yarn dresser. In an account of the part he took in the short-time question, written by himself, he says:—"I soon found that the great number of hours that the operative had to be confined to the machine, and breathing an impure atmosphere, day by day, was such as to prove destructive to health, and preclude the possibility of improving the mind to any great extent. Under this impression I joined a few good men, who were then struggling to get the hours of labour reduced. I continued to do so quietly until I came into Dukinfield, where I was solicited to join or become a member of a Short-time Committee in Ashton. After Mr. Hindley's election for Ashton, a deputation was sent to him, to ascertain if he would take charge of a Ten Hours Factory Bill in parliament. That deputation consisted of myself and the late Thomas Forbes, both of us working for him under the late Mr. Hyde. He received us in the most cordial manner, as is usual with him, but requested time to consider until six o'clock in the evening, when he would give the committee an answer. He did so. He took charge of a Ten Hours Bill. When parliament met, the committee was anxious that a delegate should be sent to London; so was Mr. Hindley; but who to send became a difficult question. At length the Rev. Mr. Stephens was proposed. I strongly objected to him, from a conviction that we ought to select an operative, whose practical story would tell more weightily with members than theory, however classical the language by which his arguments might be enforced. This view of the case was at once assented to and I was requested to go myself. I absolutely refused to do so, but have lamented ever since that I did not accept the appointment, as I feel fully convinced that many evils which originated in the choice made would have been prevented. Mr. Hindley got a bill drawn up which proposed to reduce the hours of labour upon a graduated scale, viz., half an hour per day in each year until we arrived at ten hours. This bill was submitted to the delegates then assembled in London, but it was objected to, although 170 manufacturers in Yorkshire pledged themselves to support it. This was a great error, and threw the cause back for many years.

"In 1833, Mr. Brotherton, the member for Salford, had every chance of obtaining an Eleven Hours Factory Act. The bill was prepared, and the government of that day would not have opposed it; of this I was repeatedly assured by the honourable member himself. He submitted his plan to the Short-time Committees in the manufacturing districts, coupling his information with his strong attachment to ten hours, but showing the moral impossibility of obtaining a measure of that nature. He urged upon us to take eleven hours rather than nothing. Unfortunately, his proposition was rejected, and strange to say, he was denounced as a traitor ever afterwards, which led him to be very cautious in receiving deputations of working men.

"For twelve months after Mr. Hindley's election, I met the Committee twice every week, at Mr. Grundy's, the Spread Eagle Inn, Ashton; this I did after working till near eight o'clock in the evening in a hot dressing-room, and stayed till twelve or one o'clock in the morning. For six months longer, we met once a week. These meetings I attended at my own expense, no one finding me a single penny. Although this great question was set before the public, little was done until 1844, when Lord Ashley moved and carried a resolution, 'That all young persons and women should leave work at six o'clock in the evening, beginning at six in the morning'. Sir Robert Peel's government was alarmed at this, and mustered their friends on the following evening and rescinded it.

"In 1846 the matter was again introduced in parliament by Lord Ashley. It so happened that I was then chosen to go to London by the Ashton Short-Time Committee, Mr. Hindley bearing my expenses, not a single operative, with all their professed anxiety for the Ten Hours Bill ever paid one farthing; indeed it was said that I was bribed by him to advocate an eleven hours bill. I wish here to record, in justice to the character of Mr. Hindley, that he never, under any circumstances, strove to influence me beyond my own convictions; so far from that, he earnestly sought my advice, as an operative, as to the views of working men upon the subject; and I defy any living man to prove that there were not thousands of mill workers in favour of getting a bill for eleven hours. I therefore took a part in endeavouring to obtain it, my practical knowledge leading me irresistably to the conclusion that the physical health, moral, religious, and intellectual cultivation of the masses could never progress with the long hour system."

The papers from which we have given the above extract have evidently been left in an unfinished state . . .'Demise of Mr. Thomas Pitt of Dukinfield', *Ashton and Stalybridge Reporter*, 24 July 1858

_____

Trade unions, generally weak in the textile regions and further reduced after the prosecution of the agricultural 'Tolpuddle Martyrs' in 1834, played little part in the campaign. The great exception was the Manchester-based cotton spinners' organisation, under the ever-active John Doherty (1799–1854), an Irishman who personally linked a variety of Radical and working-class movements. When, in 1835, Hindley made an attempt to take the Parliamentary leadership of the cause, Doherty and Philip Grant (d 1880), an early Manchester reformer, provoked a heated discussion among Lancashire reformers.

_____

26 . . . This is the substance of a conversation between Mr. Hindley and the delegates at the close of the meeting . . . when delegates gathered round Mr. Hindley as he stood ready to depart.

Mr. Doherty: . . . Mr. Hindley, we are all round you now. Perhaps we cannot have a better opportunity to understand each other's sentiments exactly on this question. You are perhaps not aware, Sir, that there is an opinion prevailing very generally among the operatives that you are not quite in earnest about insisting on ten hours. I hope you will not take offence at me saying this, as I only wish you to know the ground on which we stand. But as to what I have stated, I appeal to these delegates, many of whom I never saw before, to say whether or not there is a strong and rather growing feeling of distrust of your sincerity in their respective districts.—The delegates simultaneously answered that it was.

Mr. Hindley: I am obliged to you, Mr. Doherty, for mentioning this matter. It is right that I should know their opinions with regard to myself and that we should understand each other exactly. As to the ten hours, all that I can say is that I am determined to divide the House on that point. I cannot compel members to vote . . . I can only push them into a division which I shall most certainly do.

Doherty: Yes, Mr. Hindley. There are two ways of dividing: one is when a division is pressed with the hope of gaining a majority, and the other, is when it is perfectly understood beforehand that you are to be beaten and that the division is only sought to save appearances.

Hindley: You labour under a great mistake if you suppose that a division of the House is looked upon as of no consequence. When members are sitting in the House, they can express their opinions to each other freely on any question without danger to their interests, but when they are bound to divide they know their opinions are then upon record and will be seen by their constituents, and themselves, of course, held responsible.

A Manchester delegate: Gentlemen, I think it is very unfair that a gentleman like Mr. Hindley, who gives his time and attention to us gratuitously, should be subjected to these sort of charges and suspected of insincerity. What better proof can Mr. Hindley give of his sincerity than of taking up the cause, and giving up his time to it as he has done and must do.

Doherty: I did not charge Mr. Hindley with insincerity. I simply told him that opinions were abroad respecting him, without saying one word as to their truth or falsehood. I know that the doubts that are entertained on this matter tend greatly to retard the exertions that would otherwise be made for the cause, and if Mr. Hindley can only remove those doubts he will find things go on much better.

Mr. Grant: Will you promise to throw up the bill if the ten hours principle be lost?

Hindley: That I shall certainly not do. It was Lord Ashley giving up his Bill that made the present Act so objectionable. If I should give up the bill, it cannot therefore stop. It must go on and if I give it up the enemies of the measure, or perhaps some of the Ministers, would take it up and instead of giving us a better bill, they might give us a worse. I admire O'Connell. I take him to be one of the best statesmen we have. He always asks for what he should have. But if he cannot get all he wants, he takes care to secure something, more especially when he knows that by taking half, he gains strength to strive for the remainder. I mean to act on that principle.

Mr. Grant: Then Mr. Hindley will you promise us that if you lose the Ten Hours in the next session, you will go on session after session till you get Ten Hours established?

Hindley: I will.

This decision was received with great applause and the delegates present expressed themselves perfectly satisfied and all their doubts removed. *Manchester and Salford Advertiser*, 12 December 1835

One of the most important groups of supporters of factory reform was the Anglican clergy of the cotton and woollen areas. At a time when 'respectability' was essential, a clerical chairman at a rally was of major importance. Furthermore, a long line of

Anglican priests provided a corps of trained speakers, useful social and political connections, and an invaluable 'moral' aura to the crusade. Several bishops helped to arouse a Christian social concern over industrial life, but perhaps the most noteworthy and heavily involved priest was George Stringer Bull (1799–1864). An audacious, hard-working, and impoverished man, he was perpetual curate of Bierley (Bradford) when he joined the Movement in 1831. He had joined the Royal Navy at the age of 10, and was subsequently a missionery in Sierra Leone. The tough, stocky parson—'the reverend bruiser' to his opponents and 'the Ten Hours chaplain' to his friends—devoted his life in Bradford (and, from 1840, in Birmingham) to inaugurating a new form of Christian social witness. He explains his motives and beliefs in the following placard attacking the Factory Commission of 1833.

27   PROTEST OF THE REV. G. S. BULL

Addressed to the Commissioners for Factory Enquiry.

GENTLEMEN,—Having been summoned to give Evidence before the Select Committee on the Factories' Bill, I esteem it my duty upon your arrival in the Neighbourhood where I reside, to present to you, in respectful terms, my Reasons for disapproving the Commission, which you have been induced to accept.

To the Royal Authority, I bow with due reverence, and to that of Parliament, when constitutionally exercised, I would render cheerful obedience. But at the same time I would never resign or fail to exercise the privilege afforded me by the Constitution of my country, to disabuse my Sovereign when I believe him to be imposed upon, or to petition against what I considered an oppressive act of the Legislature.

Believing as I do in my conscience, that the course adopted by the King's responsible Advisers in the matter of this Commission, is of the character above described, I have discharged my duty in uniting with others to Address his Majesty and to Petition Parliament against the same.

1. *I protest against this Commission as one of the Witnesses before the Select Committee.*

The course thus adopted by the avowed Enemies of the Ten Hour Bill, places my character, and that of my fellow witnesses, in jeopardy. Our veracity may be impeached *in the dark*—but we can demand no clue by which to detect the interested and specious slanderer, over whom the constitution of your Commission most injuriously spreads the thick veil of secrecy. Our Evidence before the Select Committee was given in the presence of Enemies who cross-examined us in the severest manner, and it is all printed, all published, all open to the closest scrutiny, and if we have dealt falsely, or set down ought in malice, we are justly liable to detection. Whereas, by the Constitution of your Commission, the greatest glory of British Judicial Administration is set aside in favour of the Secrecy of a Spanish Inquisition. I assert, that to establish such a principle is virtually to destroy every constitutional security for honesty in Witnesses, and for the protection of character. It operates as a Bonus to malice, slander, imposition, and misrepresentation.

2. *I protest as a Christian Man, and as a Minister of the Church of England.*

The God whom I desire to serve is "no respecter of persons", and has told you as well as me by the mouth of Solomon, "*It is not good to have respect of persons in judgment*". Now it was palpably "respect of persons", of Rich Capitalists and their influence in Parliament which induced the ministry to sue out a Royal Commission, sanctioned by an insignificant majority of one or two in the House of Commons, to adopt a method for the trial of the cause of the rich, diametrically opposite in Constitution and character to that, which they—yes the self same parties adopted for the trial of the cause of the Poor.

I protest as a Christian Man;—

Because that Divine Redeemer and Lawgiver, who rebuked even his own disciples, when they would have kept the children from him—who pronounced twelve hours occupation to be a day's work for men—would never have suffered any Rich

Capitalist of that day to have asserted his *right* because he was rich, to work children longer than their Parents, depriving them of health, moral improvement and youthful recreation. No, Sirs, had such a right been asserted by the chiefest of all the Pharisees, neither his sleek, sanctimonious visage—his many prayers—his ostentatious alms-deeds, his broad phylacteries, nor his hoard of Gold would have obtained for him a "Commission" to redeem his respectability—to receive his evidence *in secret*, or to delay for an hour the release of those helpless ones whom the Saviour owned and blessed as a peculiarly beloved portion of his kingdom below.

As a Minister of the Church of England, I conceive it my duty to maintain the cause of the oppressed and the poor, and I regard this favourite system of *Commissions,* now so generally adopted, as so many parts of a Dexterous Conspiracy, which certain Political Philosophers are under plotting, the effect of which is, to establish the domination of wealth, and the degradation of industrious Poverty. I feel, too, that the interests of Christianity itself are betrayed, into the hands of unreasonable and wicked men, by the Judas-like conduct of many of its professors, whose capital is embarked in the Factory System, whose lips salute our altars with apparent devotion—who raise their hands in her sanctuary as if to adore, but who make them fall with tyrannous weight upon the children of the needy. Whether such bitter foes of the true Religion of Christ are shrouded in a Priestly Mantle, or dwell in those Mansions and are surrounded by those parks and lawns which the over laboured infant has enabled them to procure, my Ministerial duty to my Country is the same; and whether I regard its general prosperity, its social happiness or its religious advantage, I am bound to rebuke and oppose them.

I believe, the oppression of the Rich—of those especially who hypocritically assume a Christian profession, has done more to injure Christianity than all that Voltaire or Paine ever produced.

3. *I further Protest against this Commission in the capacity of a Religious Instructor of Youth.*

The present System of Factory Labour generally precludes the possibility of sufficient Religious or common instruction; and any limitation which involves more than 13 hours occupation (which is involved in a Ten Hour Bill) will be an intolerable Evil. I am disgusted to hear from the same quarters a great cry of exultation that "the Schoolmaster is abroad" and a greater and more sincere cry against a Ten Hour Bill. The avowed object of those who obtained the appointment of the Commission, being to set aside that benevolent measure. I recognize in you, their Representatives, and not those of our Gracious Sovereign, who has too kind a heart and too honest a mind, knowingly to authorize the object of those interested and obdurate men, to whose influence you are indebted for your appointment.

As Public Men, you are open to public Remark. Of your PRIVATE *Characters I have no knowledge, of your Motives I am no judge. I have only to wish that your next appointment may not be unconstitutional in its character, and not opposed to the interests of Religion and Humanity in its object.*

I am, Gentlemen, with all submission, yours faithfully,

G. S. BULL.

Byerley, June 4th, 1833.

P.S. The 4th of June is associated from my earliest recollections with the memory of George III, who I am sure would have wished every Factory Child in his Dominions to have TIME *to read his Bible.*

Protest of the Rev. G. S. Bull, Bradford poster, 4 June, 1833

The Ten Hours Bill In 1831 Sir John Cam Hobhouse (1786–1869) proposed a Bill to limit child labour to 64 hours weekly (excluding mealtimes). Faced by strong opposition, Hobhouse gradually withdrew, finally securing merely a minor measure affecting only cotton mills. Oastler furiously protested, calling for a 58-hour week, a cry taken up in Parliament by his Leeds friend, Michael Sadler. Samuel Kydd, an Arbroath man, Chartist and Oastler's secretary in the 1850s, here quotes the bitter correspondence between Hobhouse and Oastler.

28   Hastings, Nov. 16, 1831.

Sir,—

I beg to acknowledge the receipt of your letter, and of the *Leeds Intelligencer*, of Thursday, Nov. 10. Of my letter to Mr. Baines I have no copy; otherwise I would, with pleasure, send it to you—at the same time I think it right to inform you, that if the extracts published in the *Mercury* are not satisfactory, neither the whole letter, nor anything I have it in my power to say, would be found more acceptable.

I regret very much to perceive that the discussion on the factory system is mixed up with party politics in Yorkshire, and more especially of the town of Leeds—still more do I regret that the good operatives should have been so much deluded, either by very ignorant or designing men, as to promise themselves the accomplishment of what can never be realised. Those acquainted with the real state of the question, so far as parliament is concerned, know very well that nothing can be more idle than to talk of the possibility of limiting the hours of daily labour to ten for five days, and to eight on the Saturday—and I was, and am surprised to find, by Mr. Sadler's answer to the Huddersfield deputies, that the worthy member for Aldborough should appear to concur in views so extravagant, and which can only end in disappointment.

The deputies of the operatives who attended me during the passing of the bill, and who, indeed, framed the Act, have it in their power to lay before their constituents such information as would at once convince them how groundless, and how prejudicial to their own interests, are all such expectations; and I can assure you, Sir, that the sooner the delusion is dispelled, the more likely will the reasonable wishes of the parties concerned be fulfilled. The censures which, it seems, are passed upon those concerned in the recent Act, and more especially on myself, can proceed only from those altogether unacquainted with the circumstances of the case, and from those who know nothing of the difficulty of carrying a controverted measure through parliament. It would doubtless have been very easy to have prepared a plan which would have pleased all the operatives for the moment, and have gained much applause from their inconsiderate friends, and which would have been rejected at the very first mention of the proposal in the House of Commons. But a man who has higher objects than immediate praise, would have been highly culpable in pursuing such a course, and sacrificing an attainable good for a fleeting popularity. Certainly the present Act is far from being so extensive, either in its operation or in its restrictions, as I could wish, but it was the opinion of the deputies of the operatives, that it secured many advantages, and was a decided improvement of the former legislation on the subject. I had therefore no choice left to me, except of two modes of procedure, namely, to attempt to pass my original bill in the face of all the opposition arrayed against me and at a time when even the very forms and delays of parliament would have defeated me; or to secure so much of the Act as I could pass without opposition of any kind. I did so by waiting day after day for a favourable moment, and at last got through the stages of it at *half-past three* in the morning! ! I will leave you to judge what would have been the result, if I had attempted to force any controverted clause upon the House, any single antagonist would have objected to the *time* of the discussion, and that obstacle alone would have been quite sufficient to postpone the question from day to day, until the end of the session.

My principal opponents are the Scotch flax-factors, and the West of England woollen-factors. The latter I think I might have managed to conciliate. The former gave me no hopes of a compromise, and they sent down so numerous and influential a body of members to the House against me, that resistance was hopeless; at least, as I before said, at that period of the session, and in the then state of public business. If I should be induced to make an attempt to bring back my bill to its original shape, I shall have to encounter the same difficulties, and without appointing a select committe to examine evidence, I fear that even the very introduction of the measure would be opposed with success.

Should Mr. Sadler make the effort which he seems to contemplate, of limiting the hours of labour to ten, you may depend upon it he will not be allowed to proceed a single stage with any enactment, and, so far from producing any beneficial effects, he will only throw an air of ridicule and extravagance over the whole of this kind of legislation. I trust that, on mature reflection, that very respectable gentlemen will adopt a more useful course of conduct, and in that case he may depend upon my exertions, such as they are, to second and encourage his honourable labour.

You are welcome to give any publicity which you may think desirable to this communication, and I cannot conclude without hoping, that what I have thought right to impress upon your consideration may alter in some degree the opinions you have hitherto entertained as to the best mode of promoting the object which we have, I believe, mutually at heart. John Cam Hobhouse to Richard Oastler, 16 November 1831, quoted in 'Alfred' (Samuel Kydd), *The History of the Factory Movement from the year 1802, to the Enactment of the Ten Hours' Bill in 1847*, I, 138–41. 1857

Fixby Hall, 19 Nov. 1831.

Sir,—Accept my most respectful thanks for your letter of the 16th instant, and believe me when I assure you I feel grateful to you for the exertions you have made in behalf of poor innocent and defenceless factory children; but allow me also to state, that I exceedingly regret you felt yourself obliged to yield the sacred cause of the poor to the "cold, calculating, but mistaken Scotch philosophers", who seem, very unfortunately, to have an overwhelming influence over the government of this country. Yes, Sir, although I cannot feel otherwise than grateful to you for what you have done, I wish you had manfully met those unfeeling misanthropes (whose God is money, and whose policy is the ruin, degradation, and banishment of the poor), by sound, philosophical and Christian argument, on the arena of the House of Commons, rather than have succumbed between the Committee and the House; then I am sure the laws of this country would nevermore have been disgraced by a statute *legalising* the working

of poor little children nine years old, for twelve hours per day!
Say what we may, this is disgusting tyranny, practised under the
name of freedom, on the weakest, most innocent, and most abject
slaves. In this part of the country very great anxiety is felt on the
subject, and the friends of the children are exceedingly wishful *to
know who are their enemies.* From the general tenour of your letter
to Mr. Baines (so far as he thought proper to publish it,) we were
led to believe the 'quarter' to which you were 'obliged to listen',
must have been the government; and yet Mr. Baines says, 'the
government are not to be charged with the defeat of the measure'.
Then again Mr. Baines says, 'the Board of Trade was inclined to
support *you* until embarrassed by the members of the north'. And
you say they 'were *supported* by the Board of Trade'. Mr. Baines
afterwards adds, 'It is to the credit of Yorkshire, that none of the
opposition given to the bill proceeded from either its members or
manufacturers' . . . I happen to know that petitions were sent
against it by *some* of the manufacturers of Huddersfield, Halifax,
and Bradford; and I think Mr. Baines will not dispute that these
places are in Yorkshire. Then again, I was informed, by a most
respectable and humane manufacturer, who *supported* the bill
with very great zeal and perseverance, and at considerable expense, that Mr. Marshall, of Leeds, opposed the bill . . . It
appears to the friends of the measure essentially necessary, that
they should actually *know* their opponents, otherwise they should
never know where to direct their energies. If these men *did* oppose
the operatives, they have a right to be informed of it; they would
then be able to assist in sending *up* to parliament *interest* and
argument as strong as theirs.

That the Factories Bill should now be made a political
electioneering question cannot be a matter of *surprise*, and, I
think, is not one of *regret*. We have witnessed a friend of emanci-
pation (yourself) defeated by a certain kind of *influence*, exercised
over the feelings and judgment of the representatives of the
people . . . It is very plain that, if the friends of the measure are
not determined, when an election takes place, to send up 'a
numerous and influential body of members' in favour of the

measure, there can be no hopes of any relief. I am not aware that the question is intended to be mixed up with *general* politics, but merely so far as to *secure* votes in its favour from the new members; and I sincerely hope that no members will be returned (where the operatives have any influence, or where the hateful factory system is known) but those who are *known* to be friendly to a TEN Hours' Bill. I hope the workmen will have the wisdom not to be gulled by the terms whig, tory, or radical, but be *determined to support men who support this bill.*

I really think the 'good operatives' are quite as able to exercise a correct judgment on this question as they are on the very complicated one of 'parliamentary reform'; and you know the King himself and the government made that an 'electioneering question'. We are exhorted, I see, by Mr. Baines, to 'petition parliament'. This may be very right when we have secured good members; but if we are to have our petitions presented to a body of representatives, governed by 'the cold, calculating, but mistaken Scotch philosophers', then I fancy we might as well save ourselves the trouble and expense; and I think it is very plain, from the concluding part of your letter to Mr. Baines (if he quotes correctly), that we have no chance of 'conciliating' the Scotch members without a 'numerous and influential body of members', who will be resolved to do an act of justice to our cruelly insulted and degraded infants. I hope also the landowner, the farmer, the *little* millowner, the domestic manufacturer, the little tradesman, the shopkeeper, the mechanic, and the artisan, will ALL join us in this struggle against 'Scotch philosophy'; or they may be assured, EVERY ONE OF THEM, that the system of infantile slavery is a system of UNIVERSAL PAUPERISM; nay, thousands of them have already proved this awful truth.

I am truly sorry you despair of ever carrying a bill for '*ten* hours for five days, and eight on Saturday'. You have certainly had much experience how the '*influence*' is got up 'so far as parliament is concerned'; but we know that hitherto the operatives have *nelgected* to use *their* influence, *and we think we are their friends when we advise them to use it.* The 'Scotch philosophers' have hitherto had ALL the influence, and the poor children have only had the support of disinterested philanthropists like yourself; and besides, *we are told* that, in a reformed parliament, the people will have a more direct influence. I think, then, the friends of the measure should rejoice that the people are *determined* to make this a political (electioneering) question.

I hope the limits sought by the operatives may in the end be realised; nay, in such a case I cannot doubt, till I am informed upon what principle of religion, nature, law, or policy, a child ought to be subject to two hours' *longer* work per day than a full-grown man. When I am made wise on this point, I may perhaps doubt. But *all* the 'Scotch philosophy' can never make me *fear* the success of this measure until that question be answered, and even when that point is solved, two others will arise—*viz.*, If it be beneficial? If it be magnanimous and worthy of the bravest nation in the world?

I am not altogether ignorant of the kind of parliamentary influence which makes you doubt the *possibility* of carrying even your original measure; and I know something of the difficulties you have to encounter, yet, I have no doubt that a much more extensive measure will be adopted before many years are passed; and although, at present, the idea of working infants ONLY ten hours a day may appear ignorant, ridiculous, extravagant, idle, delusive, and impossible to the legislators of this country, I cannot doubt that, in a very short time, our legislators will hardly believe it was ever possible for a Christian parliament to refuse such an act. I anticipate with gladness the day when yourself, Mr. Sadler, and Mr. Strickland (for he is *now*, I am happy to say, a TEN hours' man), will be exerting your mighty powers of eloquence for the liberation of the most oppressed beings under the sun. The alteration would at once prevent the *unnatural* effect of increasing human labour with the *increase* of machinery; it is this circumstance, proceeding not from the *nature* of machinery, *but from the avarice of man*, which makes machinery often *appear* to be a curse. The *natural* effect of

G

machinery must be to lessen human labour; the *actual* effect, *under the present system*, is to increase it.

I rejoice that Mr. Sadler has declared himself a legislator on this subject, *in accordance with the principles of his whole life*; the declaration is founded on justice, the principles are those of truth, and *must* ultimately prevail. I am at a loss to conceive how a Ten Hours' a Day Bill can be 'prejudicial to the operatives', or how such a desire can be called 'extravagant and unreasonable'. If this measure is 'rejected at the very mention of the proposition in the House of Commons', none will regret it more than myself; but that unfortunate circumstance will not dishearten its friends. It would only spur them on to greater exertions, *and would un-doubtedly lead to certain success.* 'Immediate praise' and 'fleeting popularity' are, indeed, unworthy motives, and particularly in a legislator. So far as I have experienced, they are the *last things* a man will be troubled with, *if he pursue a straightforward course, and act upon principle.*

Your 'Cotton Act' is, I believe, an improvement, and I thank you for it; but I do wish you had debated the question in the House. I think, with Mr. Strickland, that it would have been better 'that the abandonment of the bill should have been caused by an open division'.

I must apologise for the freedom and length of this epistle, and cannot conclude without thanking you most sincerely . . . As you say that I may give any publicity I may think advisable to your communication, I shall give it, along with mine, to the editors of the newspapers. I feel there ought to be no secrets on the subject. Richard Oastler to J. C. Hobhouse, 19 November 1831: 'Alfred', op cit, I, 141–6

————

After the failure of the 1831 Bill, the factory reformers turned to a new Parliamentary champion. Hobhouse, the sophisticated, metropolitan, aristocratic Whig friend of Lord Byron, was re-placed by Michael Thomas Sadler (1780–1835), a Leeds linen merchant, High Tory, and devout Churchman. Since 1829 Sadler had successively represented the ultra-Tory Duke of

Newcastle's boroughs of Newark and Aldborough. He rejected the new liberalism in its entirety, condemning Malthusian views on population and the Poor Laws, the *laisser-faire* theories of the political economists, and an industrial society in which 'a man counted from their birth the gain he should make of his children by their labour in the accursed manufactories'. Now the prospective Tory candidate for Leeds, which was to receive Parliamentary representation under the Reform Act he had opposed, Sadler was an energetic promoter of the Ten Hours' Bill, which would restrict children to a 58-hour week. On 16 March 1832 he explained the measure in a moving three-hour speech, parts of which are quoted below. Against his wishes, he was compelled to accept an investigation by a Select Committee (over which he presided). The Committee had not concluded its deliberations when Parliament was dissolved; and in December Sadler was soundly beaten at Leeds by two strong opponents of factory reform, John Marshall (1797–1836), the son of the local flax magnate, and T. B. Macaulay (1800–59), an old opponent.

---

29 The bill which I now implore the House to sanction with its authority, has for its object the liberation of children and other young persons employed in the mills and factories of the United Kingdom, from that over-exertion and long confinement, which common sense, as well as experience, has shown to be utterly inconsistent with the improvement of their minds, the preservation of their morals, and the maintenance of their health;—in a word, to rescue them from a state of suffering and degradation, which it is conceived that the children of the industrious classes in hardly any other country have ever endured.

... the boasted freedom of our labourers in many pursuits will, on a just view of their condition, be found little more than a name. Those who argue the question upon mere abstract principles seem, in my apprehension, too much to forget the conditions of society: the unequal division of property or rather its total monopoly by the few, leaving the many nothing but what they can obtain by their daily labour; which very labour cannot become available for the purposes of daily subsistence without the consent of those who own the property of the community ... the employer and the employed do not meet on equal terms in the market of labour; on the contrary, the latter, whatever his age and call him as free as you please, is often almost entirely at the mercy of the former—he would be wholly so were it not for the operation of the Poor Laws, which are palpable interference with the market of labour, and condemned as such by their opponents ... In a word, wealth, still more than knowledge, is power; and power, liable to abuse wherever vested, is least of all free from tyrannical exercise, when it owes its existence to a sordid source. Hence have all laws, human or divine, attempted to protect the labourer from the injustice and cruelty which are too often practised upon him ...

Our ancestors could not have supposed it possible—posterity will not believe it true—it will be placed among the historic doubts of some future antiquary—that a generation of Englishmen could exist, or had existed, that would labour lisping infancy, of a few summers old, regardless alike of its smiles or tears, and unmoved by its unresisting weakness, eleven, twelve, thirteen, fourteen, sixteen hours a day, and through the weary night also, till, in the dewy morn of existence, the bud of youth faded, and fell ere it was unfolded. Oh, cursed lust of gold! Oh, the guilt which England is contracting in the kindling eye of Heaven, when nothing but exultations are heard about the perfection of her machinery, the march of her manufactures, and the rapid increase of her wealth and prosperity! ...

... Sir, children are beaten with thongs, prepared for the purpose. Yes, the females of this country, no matter whether children or grown up—I hardly know which is the more disgusting outrage—are beaten upon the face, arms, and bosom—beaten in your free market of labour, as you term it, like slaves. These are the instruments. [*Here the honourable member exhibited some black, heavy, leathern thongs, one of them fixed in a sort of handle, the smack of which, when struck upon the table, resounded through the House.*] They are quite equal to breaking an arm, but the bones of the young are, as I have before said, pliant. The marks, however, of the thong are long visible, and the poor wretch is flogged before its companions—flogged, I say, like a dog, by the tyrant overlooker. We speak with execration of the cart-whip of the West Indies, but let us see this night an equal feeling rise against the factory-thong of England ... Sir, I should wish to propose an additional clause to this bill, enacting that the overseer who dares to lay the lash on the almost naked body of the child shall be sentenced to the tread-wheel for a month, and it would be but right if the master who knowingly tolerates the infliction of this cruelty on abused infancy, this insult upon parental feeling, this disgrace upon the national character, should bear him company, though he roll to the house of correction in his chariot ... The great increase of debauchery of another kind, it would be absurd to deny; I never did hear it denied, that many of the mills, at least those in which night-working is pursued, are, in this respect, *little better than brothels* ...

The principal features of this bill for regulating the labour of children and other young persons in mills and factories, are these:—First, to prohibit the labour of infants therein under the age of nine years; to limit the actual work, from nine to eighteen years of age, to ten hours daily, exclusive of the time allowed for meals and refreshment, with an abatement of two hours on the Saturday, as a necessary preparation for the Sabbath; and to forbid all night-work under the age of twenty-one.

... I compare not the English child with the African child; but I ask this House, and his Majesty's Government, whether it would not be right and becoming to consider the English child as favourably as the African adult? You have limited the labour of the robust negro to nine hours; but when I propose that the labour of the young white slave shall not exceed ten, the proposition is deemed extravagant ...

... Another objection of some of the opposing millowners I will briefly notice. They cannot consent, forsooth, to an abridgement of the long and slavish hours of infant labour because of the Corn Laws. Why, these individuals—some of them not

originally, perhaps, of the most opulent class of the community—
have, during the operation of these laws, rapidly amassed enormous fortunes; yet, during the whole period, they could seldom
afford either to increase the wages or diminish the toil of these
little labourers, to whom, however forgetful they may be of the
fact, many of them owe every farthing they possess: they have
generally done the reverse. And they talk of Corn Laws as their
apology! This is too bad. Can any man be fool enough to suppose
that, were the Corn Laws abolished tomorrow, and every grain
we consume grown and ground in foreign parts, such individuals
would cease to 'grind the forces of the poor?'

... I wish I could bring a group of these little ones to [the] bar
[of the House of Commons]—I am sure their silent appearance
would plead more forcibly in their behalf than the loudest
eloquence. I shall not soon forget their affecting presence on a
recent occasion, when many thousands of the people of the North
were assembled in their cause,—when in the intervals of those
loud and general acclamations which rent the air, while their
great and unrivalled champion, Richard Oastler (whose name
is now lisped by thousands of these infants, and will be trans-
mitted to posterity with undiminished gratitude and affection);
—when this friend of the factory children was pleading their
cause as he alone can plead it, the repeated cheers of a number of
shrill voices were heard, which sounded like echoes to our own;
and on looking around, we saw several groups of little children,
amidst the crowd, who raised their voices in the fervour of hope
and exultation, while they heard their sufferings commiserated,
and, as they believed, about to be redressed ... *Memoirs of the Life
and Writings of Michael Thomas Sadler, M.P., F.R.S., &c.*, 337/379.
1842

———

Sadler's Bill having lapsed with the dissolution of the old Parliament and Sadler having been defeated, the Northern reformers
sent Parson Bull to London in January 1833, to select a new
Parliamentary leader. Lord Ashley, later 7th Earl of Shaftesbury
(1801–85), undertook the task, reintroducing the Bill on 5

March; but on 3 April Parliament decided that a further enquiry
was needed and set up a Royal Commission. Northern reformers,
suspicious of all attempts to defend the employers, furiously protested. A retired attorney, Geoffrey Crabtree, made an early
and typical attack on the investigation.

---

30 ... Without circumlocution, I am nearly certain that the
Factory Commission is an appointment against law, and I am
quite certain that if the law of England is to prevail, the proceedings must be quashed for their illegality ...

... In clamouring for Reform we asked for a fish—we have got
something very like a serpent . . . Your Lordship manifestly
confides too much in the unhesitating promptitude of voting
among an assembly in which the business of legislative delibera-
tion is a novelty to many of its members. The new infusion un-
happily does not suit the constitution, nor dry up the peccant
humours of the patient. It must not be disguised by us, who are
reformers in spirit and in truth, that, for the present, we have
added considerably to the average ignorance of the Lower House
—and more than that; the ignorance of the new sample is the
very worst for the purpose of legislation, that can be fostered by
the public favour. Sleek men, with purses well filled, and portly
paunches, both swelled by honest industry, are very well in their
way; they do credit to the presiding genius of the State, by proving to the world how securely people of the dullest faculties may
eat and sleep. But if they have nothing besides these ... we look
in vain for the wisdom to frame good laws, or the virtue to correct
bad ones ...

... The Factory party have broken in on the constitutional
course of justice, and the Ministry will never be able to wipe out
the stain of yielding to their unhallowed cupidity ...

... Mr. G. W. Wood, Mr. Patten, Mr. Gisborne, and Mr.
Potter treated the allegations of wasted life and health as of
secondary importance to the danger threatened to fixed manufacturing capital by a diminution of the sixth part of the labour
employed by it. The law of England refuses the evidence of parties

directly interested in the event of the suit. Geoffrey Crabtree. *Factory Commission: The Legality of its Appointment Questioned, and the Illegality of its Proceedings Proved . . . Addressed to Lord Althorp*, 5, 10–12, 19. 1833

When the Factory Commissioners, briefed largely by the Benthamite Edwin Chadwick (1800–90), reached the factory districts they met with protests, demonstrations, and obstruction from the reformers. The following extracts illustrate the organisation and propaganda of the Short Time Committees.

31 The commissioners appointed to report from this district arrived at Leeds on Monday, the 13th inst. So soon as their arrival was announced, the Short Time Committee assembled, and at 7 o'clock, accompanied by about 1,000 operatives, proceeded to deliver the protest of the committee to the commissioners; describing the object of their visit as an expensive plot to delay the passing of the great measure introduced into parliament by M. T. Sadler, Esq., and now advocated therein by Lord Ashley . . . On the Wednesday evening, however, their retreat was discovered, and considerable numbers assembled in front of the hotel. On Thursday the excitement was very great, as it was publicly announced that on the evening the factory children would assemble at 7 o'clock in the Free Market, and proceed from thence to the hotel, to present their protest against the visit of the commissioners.

. . . During the whole of the day, boys were coming to the Union Inn, head-quarters of the Short Time Committee, from the different flax and woollen mills, for slips to bind round their hats, having printed thereon 'The Ten Hours Bill'. From the feeling which they manifested in favour of that measure, it appeared unnecessary for the committee to incur much expense, or make any extraordinary efforts to collect the children together. No band was engaged, and only two flags taken out, one of which was the famous one representing the scene in Water Lane (Marshall's Mills) at five o'clock in the morning, as it was thought prudent not to make much display, lest the children should be injured by the pressure of the crowd . . . Mr. Cavie Richardson, whom the children had applied to, read their protest, to which they gave their assent by three cheers, and then proceeded to Scarborough's Hotel with an immense multitude, when six of the poor children, headed by Mr. Richardson and other friends of the Ten Hours Bill, were introduced to the commissioners. *Great Meeting in Leeds, on Thursday, the 16th of May, 1833, of the Factory Children.* Leeds, 1833

32 To the Commissioners appointed by the King to inquire into the state of Factory Labour.

Gentlemen,—We, children employed in the factories of Manchester, beg leave to present to you this our humble and respectful memorial. We implore your pity and compassion for our sufferings, for the great weight of labour thrown on our young limbs,— for the long duration of that labour daily, mostly in the close air of a heated room,—for the weakness it brings upon us while we are little, and the sickness and deformity which fall upon many of us,—for the overwhelming fatigue which benumbs our senses, and for the shutting out of any chance of learning to read and write like children of our age in other employments.

We respect our masters, and are willing to work for our support, and that of our parents and brothers; but we want time for more rest, a little play, and to learn to read and write. Young as we are, we find that we could do our work better if we were to work less time, and were not so weighed down by the long continuance of our daily toil.

We do not think it right that we should know nothing but work and suffering, from Monday morning to Saturday night, to make others rich.

Do, good gentlemen, inquire carefully into our condition. Let not a respect for wealth disguise from your view our severe wrongs, nor restrain you from declaring what measure of justice is due to us. Indeed, we tell you no lies, when we say that our bodies are wasted, and our strength sinking, under our daily

tasks; and that we are without any time for amusement or learning. Surely the King does not intend that his youngest subjects
should be worked the hardest, and suffer the most. We throw
ourselves upon your mercy and justice. Look at us, and say if it is
possible that we can be disbelieved! Do your duty faithfully to us.
Tell the King the actual state in which you find us. So shall you
cause relief to come from our rulers; and so you will be repaid by
good wishes from the grateful hearts of thousands of little children
like ourselves. 'Alfred' [Samuel Kydd], *The History of the Factory
Movement*, II, 42–3. 1857

Despite the reformers' hostility, the Commission worked quickly
and issued its first and vital report on 25 June. The recommendations did not altogether correspond with the subsequently
printed evidence, and the Commissioners complained of the
reformers' 'spirit of hostility' and 'secret' desire to limit adult
labour. Nevertheless, they proposed that children aged 9–13
should be restricted (in stages) to a 48-hour week, that education
should be provided, and that an inspectorate should be established. The Act of 1833 followed these recommendations and also
limited 'young persons' of 13–18 to a 12-hour day. It was hoped
that relays of children would be employed, thus allowing long
adult hours to be maintained. The Commission's crucial arguments are quoted below.

33 One of the great evils to which people employed in factories
are exposed is, the danger of receiving serious and even fatal injury from the machinery. It does not seem possible, by any pre-
cautions that are practicable, to remove this danger altogether.
There are factories in which every thing is done that it seems
practicable to do to reduce this danger to the least possible
amount, and with such success that no serious accident happens
for years together. By the returns which we have received, however, it appears that there are other factories, and that these are
by no means few in number, nor confined to the smaller mills, in
which serious accidents are continually occurring, and in which,

notwithstanding, dangerous parts of the machinery are allowed to remain unfenced. The greater the carelessness of the proprietors in neglecting sufficiently to fence the machinery, and the greater the number of accidents, the less their sympathy with the sufferers. In factories in which precaution is taken to prevent accidents care is taken of the workpeople when they do occur, and a desire is shown to make what compensations may be possible. But it appears in evidence that cases frequently occur in which the workpeople are abandoned from the moment that an accident occurs; their wages are stopped, no medical attendance is provided, and whatever the extent of the injury no compensation is afforded.

From the whole of the evidence laid before us, we find—

1st—That the children employed in all the principal branches of manufacture throughout the Kingdom work the same number of hours as the adults.

2d—That the effects of labour during such hours are, in a great number of cases,

Permanent deterioration of the physical constitution;

The production of disease often wholly irremediable; and

The partial or entire exclusion (by reason of excessive fatigue) from the means of obtaining adequate education and acquiring useful habits, or of profiting by those means when afforded.

3d—That at the age when children suffer these injuries from the labour they undergo, they are not free agents, but are let out to hire, the wages they earn being received and appropriated by their parents and guardians.

We are therefore of opinion that a case is made out for the interference of the Legislature in behalf of the children employed in factories.

4th—In regard to morals, we find that though the statements and depositions of the different witnesses that have been examined are to a considerable degree conflicting, yet there is no evidence to show that vice and immorality are more prevalent amongst these people, considered as a class, than amongst any other portion of the community in the same station, and with the same limited means of information ... for any evil of this kind which may nevertheless exist, the proper remedy seems to be a more general and careful education of the young people.

5th—In regard to the inquiry "in what respect the laws made for the protection of such children have been found insufficient for such purpose", we find that in country situations the existing law is seldom or never attempted to be enforced, that in several principal manufacturing towns it is openly disregarded, that in others its operation is extremely partial and incomplete, and that even in Manchester, where the leading manufacturers felt an interest in carrying the act into execution as against the evasions practised by the small mill-owners, the attempt to enforce its provisions through the agency of a committee of masters has for some time back been given up. On the whole we find that the present law has been almost entirely inoperative ... First Report from the Commissioners appointed to collect information in the Manufacturing Districts, relative to the employment of children in factories, *Parliamentary Papers*, XX, 31-2. 1833

The Factory Reform Agitation The early years of the factory reform agitation were dominated by the extrovert personality of Richard Oastler. As both demagogue and popular pamphleteer, he exercised enormous influence on the Northern working-classes. In the following extract, taken from a long pamphlet consisting of an introduction, an election address, and speeches on the 1832 West Riding election, Oastler laments Sadler's defeat and presents his own philosophy.

34 ... many, very many, of Wilberforce's enemies in 1807 are on the Anti-Slavery Committees, canting and prating about their veneration for his character and worth, who did their best and their worst to keep him out of Parliament in 1807, and many have done the same towards his early and his constant friend and supporter Sadler in 1832 ...

For a season, treachery and malice and hypocrisy have

triumphed. The voters of Leeds have listened to the voice of the tempter—they have rejected the man whose eloquence was wont to be raised in Britain's senate in defence of the poor. The unoffending and oppressed factory child has lost his disinterested advocate—the starving Irish peasant has been deprived of the eloquent assertor of his rights—the English agricultural labourer will mourn that that voice which so forcibly described his sufferings and prescribed their cure, has *by the voice of the Leeds electors* been silenced—and the poor manufacturing labourers, who have done their duty, and from distant and neighbouring towns and in Leeds itself, (having no votes themselves to give,) have prayed and petitioned by tens of thousands that the *voters of Leeds* would send to Parliament the champion of their and their children's rights, will grieve to find that their prayers and their entreaties have passed unheeded, whilst falsehood and the voice of the oppressor have prevailed. They will mourn that that man on whom their hopes were fixed, and to whom their gratitude was due and freely tendered, should have been rejected by those who pretend to be the friends of liberty and freedom, and who proudly apply to themselves the epithet of "LIBERAL". Well, who can wonder, man is only fallen man! The Jews professed much zeal for God and love for piety—and they preferred Barabbas to Jesus!

. . . I have resolved to go right on. I take the Bible, the simple Bible, with me, without either note or comment, and in spite of all that men or devils may devise against me, "I WILL HAVE THE BILL", perfectly careless whether I shall gain the victory by asserting the power of truth on the floor of the House of Commons, from the dungeon of a prison, or from the chamber of a poor-house!

. . . I am *not* of the present School of "Political Economists", "Free Traders", "Liberals", so called; "Emigration Boards and Committees" I detest—I contend that the Labourer has a *right* to live on his Native Soil; there is room enough and there may be food enough in our native Land for us all.

. . . The Altar, The Throne, and The Cottage, should share

alike in the protection of the Law; the God of the Poor will never accept incense from the *first*, nor can there be stability in the *second*, if justice and mercy be withheld from the *third*.

Now Tories, what say you? Will you go back? You cannot. "Stand still?" Impossible. Will you join the Whigs against the people? If so, you are a set of unprincipled knaves, and deserve to meet with the first reward of roguery. Will you go forward, then, hand in hand with "the people" and thus save the nation from anarchy and blood—thus secure the rights of the nobles by giving comfort, peace, and contentment to the cottage? If you follow this plan, every patriot will join you, I care not whether he be Tory, Whig, or Radical, every man who loves his country will be on your side . . .

. . . I stated distinctly that a property-tax should be instituted to pay all the expences of the nation. I think so still. (*Cheers.*) I merely mentioned property, but I ought to have said, property and machinery—I mean that kind of machinery which is worked by the individual who does not belong to it. I would not have a single machine taxed which belongs to the labourer, and which assists him in working at home . . . I think that if the machine belongs to the man who works at or with it, as, for instance, the loom of a weaver in his own cottage, that is part of his own labour, and ought, in my opinion, to be exempt from any tax, because, if it were taxed it would be equivalent to a tax upon labour. If, however, he is dragged from his cottage to work at machinery in factories, which capitalists have bought—then ought machinery to be taxed, because that becomes distinctly a monopoly of property vested in machinery. The tax upon it is neither more nor less than a property tax.

. . . The tax upon this machinery will also be a premium for the domestic manufacturer. Oh! that I could once more see that useful, that happy class of men restored to their privileges! They have been sinking as the Factory System has been rising. I have seen them drop by scores, many of them are now paupers or labourers, and many more have descended to the grave, long ere their time, weighed down by poverty and want—a broken heart has led them out of life—and now, in many cases, their poor children are the victims of the Factory System! (*Hear, hear.*) I remember the time when every part of the country was happy, when every man knew that he could go out in a morning or stop at home as he pleased, and yet earn as much as would make himself and family comfortable. I remember that time was when the child was not called upon to work from five o'clock in the morning till eight or nine o'clock at night; but when it had five or six hours a day appointed for it to work, and the remainder was for recreation and improvement. At that time, little children were treated like human beings, but now they are treated worse than Negro Slaves. (*Cheers.*)

... The great mistake in the minds of those raised above the working class is, that they think the people want plunder and anarchy. I know they want no such thing—they want peace and rest—and their rights. They want to be able to go out in a morning, get a good day's work done, and come home with a fair remuneration; and then they want to be able to keep their wages free from taxation, or to have representation; that is, they don't want the tax-gatherer to enter their houses, put his hands into their pockets, and just take as much as the Ten-pounders think proper to have, without asking their leave; they want to have a say in the matter; and I think they have as much right to look after their wages as the Ten-pounders have, and that I really believe is all they want ...

... Whenever I hear a British artizan shout "cheap foreign corn", I always fancy I see his wife pulling his coat, and hear her crying out "low wages", "long labour", "bad profits". Is not that the case? I am sure I am right; is it not so? (*Yes.*) And when I hear a large mill-owner coaxing his workpeople with a promise of "cheap foreign corn", I fancy I see him shrugging his shoulders and saying, "more work for less money, that's all". (*Laughter.*) Very well, then, my principle of legislation is this—to encourage home growth, home labour, home trade, and home consumption. (*Loud cheers.*)

... As a Tory, I have always conceived that my principles

should tend to support order and happiness in every state. The King I wish to be happy on his throne—the cottager happy in his cottage. "A place for every thing, and every thing in its place"—"Live and let live"—"A good day's wages for a good day's work." These are my mottoes; and "THE ALTAR, THE THRONE, AND THE COTTAGE" is my standing toast. This I always understood to be Toryism. If I am right, then I am a Tory; you may call me a rebel if you please. Richard Oastler. *Facts and Plain Words on Every-Day Subjects*, 3–4, 12–13, 21–2, 34–5, 43–4, 55, 57. Leeds, 1833

On 11 January 1833 the Factory Movement started its first conference at Bradford, deciding to extend the organisation and appoint a new Parliamentary leader. Oastler addressed the delegates at their last meeting, bitterly attacking Methodist and liberal opponents.

35 WESLEY would not have been silent on this question, I know he would not, nor would he have refused us his chapels; but unfortunately for Methodism, the Methodists have this night refused us a hearing in their House of God ... I do know that JOHN WESLEY, had he been on earth, would have been our mighty champion, and would have let us have his chapels, no matter who had rented the front seats in the gallery. (*Hear.*) . . . Well may [the Primitive Methodists] be called PRIMITIVE, they are more like John Wesley on this occasion than are the WESLEYANS. (*Loud applause.*) . . .

Gentlemen, we now stand upon an awful precipice. You have long been told about "Tory Traps". "Tory Trap!" exclaimed the pious Mr. Baines, and then he fancied he had proved he and the mill-owners were entitled to the earnings of the poor. Never mind him; you know what he is, and so do I. (*Laughter.*) He makes money, and so he is *wise*, and I am "mad", because I value usefulness and humanity more than gold, and because I hate cant and humbug. There is no Tory Trap laid for you now; but there is *a* trap now laid for you—It is a "WHIG TRAP." (*Hear.*) For once I'll

engage to say that I will prove to a demonstration that the trap
I am going to tell you of, is laid by "pure and real humanity".
(*Laughter.*) There is no "party" feeling in it. The "humanity" of the
Whigs—(*Loud laughter*)—the humanity of Baines—(*Loud Cheers
and Laughter*)—the humanity which fills the pocket—(*Loud
Cheers*)—not that "puling" humanity of Sadler, which leads him
to spend his nights and his days at much expense of money and
health to relieve and bless the poor; such "puling" humanity
never laid this Whig Trap, no, no, 'twas the "real" humanity, the
profitless humanity of Baines the young and Baines the old, who
when the "humane" Marshall and Macaulay and the "puling"
Sadler were in the Cloth-Hall Yard—(the moment any allusion,
however distant, was made to the sufferings of the agricultural
labourer, or of the Irish peasant, or of the poor despised Factory
Child)—in fiendish concert yelled "Ya, ya, ya" as a signal for the
disgusting shouts and laughter of the self-styled "pious" in
alliance with openly professed atheists. (*Cheers.*) What but "pure"
feelings of humanity could have induced Mr. Baines to lay a
whig-trap? And he has baited it nobly with that excellent,
amiable, and able young nobleman Lord Morpeth, to catch
you. (*Cheers.*) Richard Oastler. *Speech delivered in the Primitive
Methodist Chapel, Bowling-lane, Bradford, on Monday, the Fourteenth
of January, 1833, at a Meeting of Delegates . . .*, 2, 3. Leeds, 1833

Their Bill rejected and apparently 'outbidden in humanity' by
the 8-hour provision in Lord Althorp's Factory Act of 1833, the
greatly weakened Yorkshire reformers founded the Factory
Reformation Society in October, to continue the struggle. They
still advocated a 10-hour day for all factory workers under 21,
but they were overtaken by events. In November Robert Owen,
currently engaged in forming a 'Grand Moral Union of the
Productive Classes', founded the Society for Promoting National
Regeneration at Manchester, with a universal 8-hour policy.
Oastler and his associates refused to help, but many Lancashire
reformers rallied to the new organisation, which enjoyed a wide
though brief popularity. The Society disappeared with the
H

general collapse of Owenite organisations in 1834. Its original aims are quoted below.

———

36 *It was unanimously resolved:*

1. That it is desirable that all who wish to see society improved, and confusion avoided, should endeavour to assist the working classes to obtain 'for eight hours work the present full day's wages', such eight hours to be performed between the hours of six in the morning and six in the evening; and that this new regulation should commence on the 1st day of March next.

2. That, in order to carry the foregoing purposes into effect, a society should be formed, to be called 'The Society for Promoting National Regeneration'.

3. That persons be immediately appointed from among the workmen to visit their fellow-workmen in each trade, manufacture, and employment, in every district of the kingdom, for the purpose of communicating with them on the subject of the above resolutions, and of inducing them to determine upon their adoption.

4. That persons also be appointed to visit the master manufacturers in each trade, in every district, to explain and recommend to them the adoption of the new regulation referred to in the first resolution.

5. That Messrs. Oastler, Wood, Bull, Sadler, and others, be urgently requested to desist from soliciting parliament for a ten hours bill, and to use their utmost exertions in aid of the measures now adopted to carry into effect, on the 1st of March next, the regulation of 'eight hours work for the present full day's wages'.

Resolutions of the Society for Promoting National Regeneration. Manchester, 1833

———

The factory reform campaign was often marked (as were other contemporary agitations) by religious bitterness. Tory-Anglican and Radical-Nonconformist reformers were opposed by Liberals who generally belonged to the larger Nonconformist sects. Liberal journals such as the *Leeds Mercury, Manchester Guardian,*

Dundee Advertiser, and *Bradford Observer* strongly opposed factory reform. In 1834 Oastler hit back, in typically boisterous fashion, at an attack published in the last newspaper.

___

37 Some time ago there happened to be in Bradford, a few wealthy Millowners, (ci-devant pedlars, tinkers and tailors,) who by means of cheating and lying, had managed to scrape some thousands of pounds together;—they were remarkable for their systematic acquirement of every vice, which they attempted to colour with the name of virtue—they were practical Heathens, —but they were perpetually exclaiming—"The Temple of the Lord are we". They had obtained their wealth by overworking and by defrauding the Factory Children, and were ever ringing in our ears, "WE are the real benefactors of the poor,—WE are they who find them employment—WE gain next to nothing by our manufactures—WE generously employ these poor creatures *for the sole purpose of enabling them to live.*" They were mighty "pious" praying people, but took care their work-people should neither have time nor strength to pray!—They were "doatingly fond of Sunday School teaching", but at one time managed to work their children till within twenty minutes of twelve o'clock on Saturday nights, and had them in their mills again, just twenty minutes after twelve o'clock on Sunday nights; in the interval (on Sunday) they "prayed" with them in the school, and taught them to be very obedient to their tormentors and oppressors; and this plan was adopted, not so much for any gain of theirs, oh no, these hypocrites pretended it was *necessary* to keep these poor infant slaves at this excruciating labour just to preserve them from "bad company", and to prevent them learning "bad habits", and to make them lively and wakeful during the Sabbath— teaching! These men were great lovers of "Temperance", and in public made many speeches against drunkenness—though, in private, they were often known to be "beastly drunk". They were extremely "virtuous", but some how, they could not be satisfied with the society of their own wives, occasionally they attacked the virtue of their poor, defenceless, mill-girls;—nay, sometimes they took a jaunt of a few weeks with them, to have them all to themselves, far from wife and home!—and it is a fact, some of the children, the fruits of these illicit intercourses, are now working as Factory Children in their father's mills!—whilst others have been "worked out", beyond their strength, and are at this moment *kept* in work-houses, at the expense of the townships! ! !

This is the real character of these "pious" *dissenting* "saints" ... Richard Oastler. *A Letter to Those Sleek, Pious, Holy and Devout Dissenters, Messrs. Get-All, Keep-All, Grasp-All, Scrape-All, Whip-All, Gull-All, Cheat-All, Cant-All, Work-All, Sneak-All, Lie-Well, Swear-Well, Scratch-Em and Company, The Shareholders in the Bradford Observer, in Answer to their Attack on Richard Oastler in that Paper of July 17, 1834,* 3. Bradford, 1834

By 1836 many reformers were convinced that local justices were tolerating breaches of the Factory Act by their manufacturer friends, while dealing harshly with proletarian offenders. When Liberal Leeds magistrates let a master off with a caution after imprisoning the Radical Joshua Hobson (1811–76) for selling 'unstamped' newspapers, Oastler issued the following protest to the Mayor, George Goodman (1792–1859) on 11 September. At Blackburn four days later he threatened to wreck machinery if evasions continued.

------

38   ... The people are tired of seeing unstamped sellers, and poachers, sent by wholesale to prison; and then *five shillings*, and *ten shillings*, and *twenty shillings*, allowed to be paid as the price of "Child murder". I say, Sir, the people are weary; they are sick of this child's play at Justice ...

... There is no meanness, no dishonour [that some employers] will not stoop to, in order to entrap a child ... Bless your life, my friend, some of these first-rate "canters", these liberal, Dissenting deaconized blood-hounds, used, before they put the breaking-bits on, to work the poor infant slaves till within twenty minutes of the Sabbath morn—and as soon as the clock struck twelve on Sunday night, the Slaves were at their mills again! But Sunday

was a Holy Day! oh! how they prayed, and wept, and canted!—
Six days they lied and cheated, and murdered, but the Seventh,
they did keep Holy, excepting that the Mechanics, and Joiners,
& Chimney Sweepers, were, all Sabbath Day long as busy as
Bees, mending, repairing, and sweeping in their Mills! But what
of that? They, the Masters, were signing Petitions to have the
Sabbath kept Holy; they were storming against Negro Slavery;
and were subscribing to the Missionary Society, and so forth.

... I never see one of these pious, canting, murdering, 'liberal',
'respectable' saints, riding in his carriage, but I remember that
the vehicle is built of infants' bones; that it is lined with their
skins; that the tassels are made of their hair; the traces and har-
ness of their sinews; and that the very oil, with which the wheels
are greased, is made of Infants' Blood!

... Mr. Mayor, do you think that the people will long remain
still? That the Giant will always slumber? Do you suppose that
Labour will always lay prostrate in the presence of Capital? Do
you really fancy, that the people are such perfect dolts, as by their
Labour to support a system, which only enslaves them, and
enriches their oppressors? A system which defies Law, and per-
verts Justice? Are you really so foolish? If so, *sleep on*!—I hope
to see Labour stand upright. I hope to see a labouring man stand
at the Bar of Justice, as free from fear, as the man of wealth. I hope
to see a race of Magistrates who shall be as polite to the poor man,
as to a rich one—as fearless and as constant in punishing a man
of wealth, as a poor poacher.

... Be warned in time—pervert the Laws no more in favour of
the 'respectables'. You cannot keep labour down, if you try,
much longer; and if some of us must be 'bulletted' by these
hateful monsters, we shall soon have bloody times.

One thing is clear, either that the Factory System must be
'uprooted from its source', as GREG has it, or that the Factory
Law must be enforced. That shall be true, Mr. Mayor.

... In the name of some Hundreds of Thousands of Working
Men, I demand the full enforcement of the Factories' Law—
against Rich, and against Poor. I demand it of you. I demand

it of the Bench everywhere.—If it is still allowed to sleep, expect the Giant to awake,—and that right suddenly. Richard Oastler. *The Unjust Judge, or the 'Sign of the Judge's Skin'. A Letter to George Goodman, Esq., Mayor of Leeds, on his Worship's Recent Refusal to Imprison a Criminal under the Factories' Regulation Act*, 7–10, 12. Leeds, 1836

Joseph Rayner Stephens (1805–79) was a Methodist minister who was expelled by the Connexion in 1834 for his anti-Establishment activities. He set up as an independent preacher, with several congregations in the Ashton-under-Lyne district. A Tory-Radical demagogue, he joined the Factory Movement 'officially' in 1836 and was thereafter a militant opponent of industrial conditions and the New Poor Law. He became increasingly violent, particularly in speeches against the Poor Law: 'the law of devils . . . ought to be resisted to the death'. Though never a Chartist, he surpassed most ultra-Radicals in the revolutionary fervour of his oratory, which was liberally spiced with Biblical references. Arrested in December 1838, he was sentenced to 18 months' imprisonment in August 1839 for addressing a seditious meeting at Hyde. In January he had explained his case.

39 . . . The battle we are now fighting from one end of England to the other is not the battle which most men take it to be. It goes much further—it runs much deeper than most men have ever yet supposed it to do. It is not a battle of party against party for the time being. It is not a struggle for power or for place among men who, for the moment, are placed in antagonistic relation to each other. It is the working of the mystery of iniquity mentioned in Holy Scripture—the mystery of ungodliness—the battle directly though not ostensibly—the struggle actually though not openly avowed—the struggle particularly of Christ in his spirit, is wielded against Belial in his spirit, and his spirit in his children. It is the battle between God and Mammon—between Christ, the Prince of Peace, and Belzebub, the Prince of the Devils. The question is, whether God shall reign in England, or whether Satan shall domineer—the question is whether the laws of Heaven and the institutions of mercy are to be the laws of a Christian land, and the institutions of a Christian people; or whether laws begotten below and born here on earth are to be the laws and institutions to which a once Christian land, and a once Christian people, are to be compelled to submit. It is the battle, my brethren, of this book (the Bible) against the earth and against hell. If this book stands, they fall.—(Several voices, "Just so"). If this book falls, great is the fall of the House of God, and you will be buried in the ruins. The lists are drawn—the battle is set—the field is pitched—deadly will be the struggle; and who is able—who feels himself able, to enter into that warfare? Pray God that he will teach your hands to war and your fingers to fight. I am well aware, my brethren, that I have long been charged—indeed, have always been charged, with a deviation—a departure from the duties prescribed to the profession of which I am an unworthy member, though I trust an upright, a sincere, and devoted one. I have been charged with departing from the duties of that profession, by wandering away to what have always hitherto been considered the forbidden paths of politics, by the introduction into my discourses of subjects which I am sorry to say, for so many years, if not ages, have always been considered as foreign from the pulpit; and as it may happen that the bonds by which you and I have been held together now some years, in love and brotherly kindness, may be broken asunder—as it may happen, and before very long, that you and I will have to bid one another farewell, it's only right to you and myself, and to the truth, whose interpreter I am—to the book whose expounder I have endeavoured to be—and to the service and master, whose Minister I am—it's only right that I should this day, in the opening service of the New Year, again repeat what I have so often asserted, that unless a priest, minister, clergyman, religious teacher—call him what you like—unless a priest of the living God be a politician in the pulpit, he has no business there at all.—(Several voices, "No, he has not".) Law and religion can never be separated. If you attempt to dissociate them, or to disunite them, it is like attempting to dissociate and disunite the soul from the body of man, and expect, after you have done so, to find a living being before you. The body without a spirit, is dead—faith without works, is dead—politics without religion, is dead—religion without politics, is dead—the one is the body, the other is the soul. [J. R. Stephens]. *A Sermon preached by the Reverend Mr. Stephens, in his Chapel at Charlestown, on Sunday, January 6, 1839; being the First Sabbath after his Release from the New Bailey at Manchester*, 4. 1839

The Propaganda Battle   A huge amount of propaganda was issued during the course of the factory agitation. One of the most effective pamphlets was published in 1836 by John Fielden (1784–1849), a major cotton manufacturer at Todmorden and Radical MP for Oldham from 1832 to 1847. The son of a self-made yeoman-manufacturer, Fielden had worked in the family mills from the age of ten. An admirer of Cobbett (his fellow-Member until 1835), he supported Ashley's Bill and Owen's National Regeneration Society, strongly opposed the New Poor Law, and financed part of the Lancashire agitation. He staunchly supported Oastler and in 1836 was incensed by the proposal of C. E. Poulett Thomson (1799–1841) to restrict the operation of the 8-hour day to children under 12. In 1846 Fielden succeeded Ashley as the Parliamentary leader; and his Conservative sons, Samuel (1816–89), John (1822–93), and Joshua (1827–87) continued his work. The following quotation from 'Honest John's' most popular publication represents the views of a leading reformer who was also a major industrialist.

40   When I consented to become a Member of Parliament, it was not with a view of joining party men or aiding in party movements; but, in order to assist, by my role, in doing such things as I thought would benefit the labouring people as well on the land as in the factory and at the loom. I have, all my years of manhood, been a Radical Reformer, because I thought

Reform would give the people a power in the House of Commons that would secure to them that better condition of which they are worthy.

There is no natural cause for our distresses. We have fertile land, the finest herds and flocks in the world, and the most skilful husbandmen; we have fine rivers and ports, and shipping unequalled; and our ingenuity and industry have given us manufactures which ought to complete these blessings. I am a manufacturer; but I am not one of those who think it time we had dispensed with the land. I think that these interests are all conducive to the prosperity of the nation; that all must go together, and that the ruin of either will leave the others comparatively insecure.

But, with all our means of prosperity, and, if we believe the high authority which reminds us of it every session of Parliament, with all the prosperity that we *have*, I cannot believe it necessary that the manufacturers should work their labourers in the manner that they do. The proposition, therefore, of my *Lord Ashley*, to diminish the excessive labour of those who work in factories, is one for which I cordially thank him, and in which he shall have my support. I know it to be one of bare justice and humanity. I have long thought it, and have aided those who were more active than myself in attempts to obtain it. I am concerned in a very large business myself, and as my manufacture, my home trade and my export trade, is almost exclusively of that sort in which the Americans attempt to compete with us, I must be one of the first to be ruined, if foreign competition is to ruin it.

The object of the following pages is to show that the workpeople have been and are cruelly treated; that they have not idly asked for protection, but that humanity and justice require it; that we shall do ourselves no harm by granting it to them; but always avowing, that I would cast manufactures to the winds, rather than see the workpeople enslaved, maimed, vitiated, and broken in constituion and in heart, as these pages will but too amply prove they now are.

JOHN FIELDEN

London, *17th May*, 1836

. . . [In 1833 the Government] were in this dilemma: the Committees had always discovered the same cruelties in practice; the same overworking, and the same horrifying results . . . They could not refuse to protect the children. But they are 'political economists'; and though, *as men*, they could no longer screw up their minds and hearts so far as to sacrifice any more limbs and lives of infants, the science would not suffer them to invade the 'freedom of industry', by involving the adult in that protection which they were obliged to give to the child. It is this absurd attempt to separate the adult from the child in its labour, that has rendered every Act that has ever been passed to give protection to children, almost void; and it is only by forcing the masters to obey this Act now in existence, that will bring *them*, and after them the *Government*, to yield to the really practicable and salutary measure that the whole of the factory labourers require at their hands. [The Inspectors] . . . amuse themselves in writing up to the Government, suggestions, that a short Act may be passed to carry us back not to the time proposed by Lord Ashley, but to that of Sir John Hobhouse's Act.

. . . The Ministers stand, therefore, in this position: they threw out Lord ASHLEY's Ten-hour Bill, because Commissioners of their own told them it did *not give protection to children*, whose labour ought to be restricted to eight hours. Then, as their Eight-hour Act will not work pleasantly, upon the advice of their Inspectors, they want to drive us back to *twelve hours*, because *that is adequate protection*!

But, we, who contend for a Ten-hour Bill, are now just where we were when the Ministry began to dabble officiously in affairs which it did not understand. . . .

I well remember being set to work in my father's mill when I was little more than ten years old; my associates, too, in the labour and in recreation are fresh in my memory. Only a few of them are now alive; some dying very young, others living to become men and women; but many of those who live have died off before they attained the age of fifty years, having the appearance of being much older, a premature appearance of age which I verily believe was caused by the nature of the employment in which they had been brought up. For several years after I began to work in the mill, the hours of labour in our works did not exceed *ten* in the day, winter and summer, and even with the labour of those hours, I shall never forget the fatigue I often felt before the day ended, and the anxiety of us all to be relieved from the unvarying and irksome toil we had gone through before we could obtain relief by such play and amusements as we resorted to when liberated from our work. I allude to this fact, because it is not uncommon for persons to infer that, because the children who work in factories are seen to play like other children when they have time to do so, the labour is, therefore, light, and does not fatigue them. The reverse of this conclusion I know to be the truth. I know the effect which ten hours' labour had upon myself; I who had the attention of parents better able than those of my companions to allow me extraordinary occasional indulgence. And he knows very little of human nature, who does not know that, to a child, diversion is so essential, that it will undergo even exhaustion in its amusements. I protest, therefore, against the reasoning that, because a child is not brought so low in spirit as to be incapable of enjoying the diversions of a child, it is not worked to the utmost that its feeble frame and constitution will bear . . .

. . . But the overworking does not apply to children only; the adults are also overworked. The increased speed given to machinery within the last thirty years, has, in very many instances, doubled the labour of both . . .

. . . We have nothing to fear from foreign competition. It is the greatest humbug that Englishmen were ever made to believe in; but from competition amongst ourselves we have everything to fear; and if we do not restrain ourselves in time, or the legislature do not restrain us, we shall very soon destroy ourselves . . .
John Fielden. *The Curse of the Factory System; or a short account of the origin of factory cruelties; of the attempts to protect the children by law; of their present sufferings; our duty towards them; injustice of Mr.*

Thomson's bill; the folly of the Political Economists; a warning against sending the children of the South into the factories of the North, iii–iv, 17–18, 24, 31–2, 35, 61. 1836

Dr Charles Wing (1793–1869) of the Royal Metropolitan Hospital for Children maintained an old tradition among socially conscious doctors by supporting shorter industrial hours. In 1836 he wrote in *The Lancet*—then run by the Radical MP Thomas Wakley (1795–1862)—of the bad health caused by industrial conditions in Manchester. In 1837 he published a selection of Parliamentary evidence on factory conditions. His introduction explained his views.

41 Dissertation on the Evils of the Factory System.

The object of the present publication is to prevent, as far as bringing evidence within the reach of the public can do so, a partial return to the factory system, as it existed previously to the year 1833, since a partial return to that system is in itself an evil, and may be the prelude to a total return . . .

. . . The Ministers . . . threw out Lord Ashley's ten-hours bill at the recommendation of their own commissioners, who gave it as the result of the evidence they had collected, that the labour of children ought to be restricted to eight hours, and that, therefore, a ten-hours bill would not afford them sufficient protection. And now these same ministers would drive back a large proportion of these children to twelve hours . . . Ministers bring in an inefficient bill, and 35,000 children are to suffer for it.

. . . Ministers found themselves in a dilemma; either they must overwork the children, or underwork adults,—and they have got out of the dilemma by determining to overwork the children. In their alarm they have thrown consistency overboard; and the very same men who declared even ten hours' labour too long for a child in his thirteenth year, would now expose him to be worked twelve hours.

. . . The vigilance of the inspectors is not a match for the money-getting spirit of the masters, and the stimulating effect of higher wages upon the workmen. The apparatus for carrying the present Act into effect is palpably inadequate; the few inspectors and superintendents that are appointed would need the eyes of Argus, the hands of Briareus, and the seven-League boots of Jack the giant-killer, with his coat of invisibility, to discharge their duties effectually . . . The present Act enlists so many interests against itself, that it has been, and will continue to be, defied or evaded . . .

. . . The commissioners object to the ten-hours bill, that it does not accomplish the object at which it purports to aim. Its professed object is the protection of children; but it does not protect children. Now all I contend for is, that it would protect children better than the present act . . .

. . . I find in [Andrew Ure's] works such an account of [the factory system], that, if I did not think the Doctor's judgment to be biassed by his prepossessions, and if I could by any possibility keep out of consideration the length of the hours of labour, I should wish it perpetual. Skipping the Inferno, and the Purgatorio, he calls the attention of his readers to the Paradiso of the system, and the reader of Dante, who should confine his attention to the third great division of his work, would form as correct a notion of the whole as the reader of Dr. Ure's publications would of the factory system from the Doctor's account of it. Charles Wing. *Evils of the Factory System demonstrated by Parliamentary Evidence*, i, ii, xxvii, xxxvii, xlix. 1837

————

Leonard Horner (1785–1864), a member of the Factory Commission in 1833, succeeded a Mr Musgrave as Factory Inspector for Scotland, Northern Ireland, Cumberland, Westmorland, Durham and Northumberland. A graduate of Edinburgh University, geologist, FRS, partner in the family linen enterprise, and (in 1828–31) warden at London University, he was the most famous and most active of the four Inspectors. In 1836 he succeeded Robert Rickards as Inspector in Yorkshire, Lancashire, Cheshire, northern Derbyshire, Staffordshire, and parts of Wales. His enormous area was reduced in 1837; thereafter he worked mainly in Lancashire, until his retirement in 1858. Like his colleagues, he inevitably supported the Act of 1833; but experience led him to favour further government intervention, still being suggested by Ashley in the late 1830s. Horner honestly revealed his views when introducing a comparative survey of different nations' policies in 1840.

---

42 It is hoped that Parliament, during the present Session, will be again called upon to legislate in behalf of the children employed in factories; and, for the sake of the many who are unprotected in consequence of the defects in the existing law, as well as for the sake of the honest mill-owner who strictly obeys the law, but is exposed to unfair competition from the too easy evasions of it by his less scrupulous neighbours, it will be a matter of great regret if another session should be allowed to terminate without an amending Act having passed . . .

The Act of 1833 has been productive of much good: it has put an end to a large proportion of the evils which made the interference of the legislature then necessary. But it has not done nearly all the good that was intended; it has not by any means accomplished all the purposes for which it was passed. The failures have mainly arisen from defects in the law itself; not in the principles it lays down, but in the machinery which was constructed for the purpose of carrying the principles into operation . . . it was in some degree legislating in the dark; a great part of the mechanism adopted was entirely of a novel description, of a kind that had never been tried in former factory acts; and after it was set to work, much of it was found to have been ill-contrived, and some positively so bad that it obstructed, and to a great degree prevented, the attainment of the object. Many, and some of the worst, of the defects cannot be laid to the charge of the original framers of the Bill, but were caused by the interference of members who were not aware what they were doing, and who were, in most instances, prompted by others. It was very natural, and it was to be expected, that the mill-owners should be stirring at such a moment, and that they should endeavour to make the law press as lightly as possible upon themselves. But too much weight was attached to their broad assertions, (much more than the parties themselves would now claim for them), that if such and such things were done, the most serious consequences would ensue to the manufacturing interest, the great strength of the country. They spoke with the confident tone of superior knowledge and experience; used technical terms, unintelligible, and, therefore, having a somewhat mystical import to those they were addressing; and the legislators, with a very natural timidity and caution, did not venture to disregard altogether remonstrances so strongly made . . .

. . . Government were applied to, to prevent the impending evil; the inspectors were appealed to by the Government, and they stated that the assertions had been so often and so confidently made to them, that they could not venture to set up their opinions and their then limited experience in opposition to them. The President of the Board of Trade, Mr. Thompson, was prevailed upon to propose to Parliament that the restriction to eight hours' daily work should be limited to children under twelve years of age; but happily Parliament was firm, and would not yield. And what was the result? Not a single mill throughout the United Kingdom stopped a day for want of hands . . .

It will be of great consequence to look with a jealous eye upon all proposed changes of phrases, and even of single words, by interested parties. They may seem harmless to those unacquainted with the practical working of the act; but they may have this effect, as we know by experience, that an important enactment may thereby be rendered inoperative . . .

The defects of the existing law have been repeatedly pointed out by the inspectors in their reports; and the Bill that was brought in by Government last year, but withdrawn on account of the then advanced period of the session, remedied nearly the whole of these defects; although, in my opinion, not all of them, nor in the best way. The evidence given before the Committee, now sitting, has made the imperfections still more apparent; and there is, therefore, every reason to expect, that a much better

Act will be obtained than would have passed before this late inquiry took place. Judging from the Government Bill of last year, it is not very probable that any material extension of the principles of the present Act will be made, except in the case of silk mills . . . There never was any sound reason for these exemptions *in favour of silk mill-owners*, and there is none now. If the question were, "What does the interest of the silk mill-owners require?", and if the labour of the children were to be accommodated accordingly, we know very well what the answers of the masters would be; but the question to be asked is: "What does the interest *of the children* require?" And Parliament must tell the masters, that they must accommodate themselves the best way they can to the conditions upon which alone the State will allow them to purchase infant labour; and those conditions must be such as will effectually protect the health of the children, and secure some education for them; but, at the same time, with as little inconvenience as possible to them, as to all other mill-owners, and to the workers of all ages employed in the factories...

. . . I have heard it said that to interfere to the extent here proposed would be humanity running riot, and exceeding all reasonable bounds; that it would be an encroachment on parental rights, and would be at variance with all sound principles of legislation. So far from thinking this to be the case, it appears to me that the interposition of the legislature in behalf of children is justified by the most cold and severe principles of political economy; and the alleged interference with parental authority by such legislation is a mere sophism.

The wealth of a country surely depends, in no inconsiderable degree, on the people who are engaged in works of industry, being capable of performing the greatest possible amount of labour in a given time, without impairing their health; for it will cost a great deal less to maintain, in food, clothes and lodging, two strong healthy men employed to perform a piece of work, than would be required if we had to employ three men to do the same work, because of their inferior muscular powers. To cultivate the intelligence, and increase the probability of useful inventions, by improving the natural faculties of the working classes, must also be considered a source of national wealth; and to be spared the expense of the repression and punishment of crime seems no less clearly an important element in national prosperity ...

... If the father has his natural rights, so has the child; and if the father robs him of these, the State must become his guardian, and restore them to him ... The increasing tendency to employ children, and for such a number of hours daily as is ruinous both to their physical and moral condition, in order to cheapen production, in almost all branches of industry, and the growing, unnatural, and vicious practice of parents making their children work, to enable themselves to live in idleness and profligacy, can only be checked by some law of general application. Leonard Horner. *On the Employment of Children, in Factories and Other Works in the United Kingdom, and in Some Foreign Countries*, v, 1–7, 15–16, 18. 1840

Much of the 'grass-root' argument over factory reform was carried on by local controversialists. Letters to the press, reprints of newspaper reports, and placards and pamphlets of various sizes formed the bulk of the Movement's propaganda efforts. The following poster issued by reformers in Pudsey (where a committee was formed in 1833, with the help of the Vicar, David Jenkins) is a good example of such local efforts.

43   THE FACTORY BILL
Fellow Countrymen and Fellow Christians,
You are respectfully invited to the Meeting, to be held on Thursday Evening next at Half-past Seven o'Clock, in the CHURCH Sunday-School ROOM, at Pudsey.

The object of the Meeting is to secure TIME for Rest, and for play—[yes, for play]—for Fire side Improvement—for Domestic Improvement—for Literary Advancement by Evening Schools, and, above all, for Religious Instruction to all Factory Workers.

The means we propose is, to prevent all Repeal of the present

I

Act, un..
ti...

..til the Legislature will give us, instead of it, a good effec-
.e TEN HOURS' BILL.

Are you a parent? Then you ought to come and speak a word, or
at least hold up two hands, for those over-laboured and un-
instructed youth that crowd the Mills.

Are you an Overlooker? Then come and imitate those 80 Overlookers at Keighley, and those 156 Overlookers at Bradford, who
have petitioned for a Ten Hours' Bill—They have done themselves great credit—they have shewn Christian benevolence,
and good British Independence.

Are you a Slubber? Why should you oppose a Ten Hours' Bill.
You would be all the better for it. When Slubbers are *in demand*
their wages rise, as well as the Children's—and when they throw
each other out of work by working too long, then their wages fall.
Is not Ten Hours long enough? *What nonsense it is to cry out, "If
you have only TEN Hours' work you must be content with TEN Hours'
Wages"*—that is with one sixth less. Let those who raise this silly
cry first prove, that the Operatives *now* get, for *twelve* hours, such
wages as they *ought* to have for *twelve* hours' *work*. That's the first
thing to prove. The fact is *they don't get their share of their own productions*, and they never will get it, till they shorten time, and
make Human Labour prizable and valuable. Restriction, so far,
has raised wages, and will do so again. The longer you have
worked, the less you have had in proportion.

Are you an Employer? Surely you have tasted the good effects of
the present Act. How steady has Trade been! How good have
Profits been! And where are all the Prophecies about Ruin and
Distress? So *far* then Restriction has proved a safe Experiment.

But, Sir, is not TEN hours long enough for any MAN to work,
and say nothing about *Children?* And would not your workpeople
be able to learn their duty to *you*, as well as to God, much better
if they gave over at six every night, and worked only Ten Hours?
And then *you* yourself would have more time to learn *your* duty
too, and to cultivate the friendship of your servants. You and
your people would be better friends.

Perhaps you belong to that Class of Employers who are joined in

Companies. That Class has happily increased of late, and nothing has increased them more, than the present Act, which has prevented night work, and the practice of 14 or 16 hours work, when trade was plentiful. Why, friends, you surely do not want, now that *you* have got up, to kick the ladder down? If this be your intention, it is to be hoped, that those who are expecting one day to be Masters as you are, will take care to keep the Ladder up, and to make it wider, by a Ten Hours' Bill.

Don't you all know that if a slack trade comes, for one three Months, one half of the small Mill Masters, who are *new beginners*, will be smashed to pieces? And what then is to prevent a slack time? Nothing but shorter hours. Mills are increasing, and Machinery is extending rapidly on every side, and in twelve months from this time, if you do not lessen the hours of work, *you* will be in a bonny mess. YOU HAVE NO NEED TO WORK SO LONG FOR A GOOD LIVING. Work a reasonable time, and you will do well. Work and think. Work and improve your minds. Save TIME for this, and save Bodily and Mental Energies for this. Remember, ye are Men and not Brutes.

Are you a Minister of the Gospel? Then imitate the Good Samaritan, and do not, like the Priest and the Levite, pass by on the other side. Perhaps you say the Advocates of the Ten Hours' Bill *are not judicious*—then do you come, Rev. Sir, and put us into a better way, we most respectfully intreat. We will respect your office, and hear your advice.

Are you a Man? Then shew your nature, and sympathise with the sorrows and disadvantages of Childhood and Youth. WAS MAN ONLY MADE TO LABOUR?

Are you a Woman? Then come to the Meeting: it is for all that have hearts to feel, and if *you* have not, you are not *a Woman.*

"But I am a Factory Child". Then come Factory Children, we will make room for you—you are welcome, always welcome to
THE FRIENDS OF THE TEN HOURS' BILL.
April 9th 1836.
Pudsey Short Time Committee poster, 1836

The Later Movement   Parliamentary discussions of further factory reform in 1838, 1839, and 1841 achieved nothing. At the General Election of 1841 many northern Chartists and factory reformers supported the Conservatives under Sir Robert Peel, 2nd baronet (1788–1850). The northern Tories' heavy involvement in the cause led such men to expect action over the factory and Poor Law issues from Peel's new Government, but Peel and his Home Secretary, Sir James Graham (1792–1861), after initial vagueness let Ashley know (in January 1842) that they could not support a Ten Hours' Bill. Ashley immediately informed his supporters.

---

44   London, February 2, 1842.
Gentlemen,

It is with the deepest regret that I am obliged to announce to you that Sir Robert Peel has signified his opposition to the Ten Hours' Bill; and I conclude therefore, as you will conclude, that his reply must be taken as the reply of the whole Government on this important question.

Though painfully disappointed, I am not disheartened, nor am I at a loss either what course to take, or what advice to give— I shall persevere unto my last hour, and so must you; we must exhaust every legitimate means that the Constitution affords, in petitions to Parliament, in public meetings, and in friendly conferences with your employers—but you must infringe no law, and offend no proprieties; we must all work together as responsible men, who will one day give an account of their motives and actions; if this course be approved, no consideration shall detach me from your cause—if not, you must select another advocate.

I know that, in resolving on this step, I exclude myself altogether from the tenure of office; I rejoice in the sacrifice, happy to devote the remainder of my days, be they many or be they few, as God in his wisdom shall determine, to an effort, however laborious to ameliorate your moral and social condition.

I am, gentlemen,
Your faithful friend and servant,
ASHLEY.
Lord Ashley to the Short Time Committees, 2 February 1842

The industrial riots of 1842 led Graham to speed up his plans for further factory legislation. In March 1843 he proposed a Bill limiting children aged 8–13 to 6½ hours' daily labour, with 3 hours' education. The predominantly Anglican control of the new factory schools—urgently needed though they were and despite the existing lead of the Church of England and its National Society—led dissenters to strong protests, and the proposal was withdrawn. In February 1844 Graham introduced another Bill, limiting children to 6½ hours and women to 12 hours' work, but dropping the educational clauses. Ashley sought to engraft a 'Ten Hours' clause, but after initial success was defeated by ministerial threats of resignation. The following notice by the Keighley committee is typical of the Northern reformers' publicity.

---

45 TEN HOURS' FACTORY LABOUR.

AT A MEETING,
Of the Short Time Committee of Keighley, in the West Riding of the County of York, held on Friday Evening, March 8th, 1844, the following resolution was unanimously adopted, to which we beg respectfully to draw your attention, in the hope that you may be pleased to give to Lord Ashley your cordial support in the effort he is about to make to obtain a Law to protect Young Persons employed in Factories, from being worked in them more than Ten Hours per Day for Five Days in the Week, and Eight on the Saturday.
JOSEPH VICKERS, Secretary.
Resolved—That this Meeting is deeply convinced that the just claims of the Factory Population require that the Hours of Labour for all Young Persons under 21 Years of Age, employed in Factories, should be limited to *Ten* per day, for Five days of

the Week, and *EIGHT* on Saturday. Keighley Short Time
Committee circular to Members of Parliament. March, 1844

Although Graham's Act was an important gain, starting the
children's 'half-time system' and restricting women's work, the
reformers were in a bitter mood after their Parliamentary defeat
in 1844. Some favoured local compromises and negotiations with
employers, and others blamed Ashley for not introducing his
Bill once more. A conference of thirty-two delegates was summoned by the following notice, to decide the Movement's policy.
A majority supported Ashley's tactics.

46 THE TEN HOURS' BILL

To the Factory Operatives of the United Kingdom
Fellow Operatives,

The position of the Ten Hours' Bill at the present period is
such as to require your most serious attention. The introduction
of the measure into Parliament this session is surrounded with
numerous difficulties, which it is your duty promptly to consider.
With a view therefore of ascertaining the opinions of the factory
workers, the Lancashire and Yorkshire Central Short-Time Committees have deemed it right to convene a Meeting of Delegates
from every town in the manufacturing districts, to consult together and determine what is the best course to be adopted under
existing circumstances. On Sunday, June 8th, 1845, a Meeting
of Delegates will therefore be held at the York Tavern, York
Street, Todmorden, at Eleven o'clock, to which meeting every
district is particularly requested to send, at least, one delegate.
May 31st 1845

Signed, H. Green, Sec., Lancashire.

M. Balme, Sec., Yorkshire.

Central Short Time Committees notice, May 1845

From prison Oastler continued to watch and comment on cur-
rent politics. Northern supporters constantly sent him gifts, but
years in the Fleet and Queen's Prisons gradually eroded his

health. In November 1843 an 'Oastler Liberation' campaign began at Huddersfield. Backed by such men as John Fielden, John Walter (1776–1847)—the owner of *The Times*—the 2nd Lord Feversham (1798–1867), and a host of other 'Ten hours' veterans, Ferrand started a Tory-Radical campaign to raise funds to pay off Oastler's debts and secure his release. Oastler was liberated in 1844, in time to participate in a new and almost successful campaign. Parliamentary discussion was reopened by Ashley in January 1846, but, shortly afterwards, as a supporter of Peel's decision to repeal the Corn Laws, Ashley felt morally bound to resign his Protectionist seat. Fielden then assumed the leadership, supported by Protectionists, Whigs, and Radicals. In May the Ten Hours' Bill was rejected by 203 votes to 193. The narrowness of the defeat encouraged reformers to renew their agitation during the winter of 1846–7. Ashley gave the news to the north in the following letter.

47   LONDON, May 27th, 1846.
GENTLEMEN,
After three successive debates of great power of interest, a majority of ten, in a house of four hundred members, rejected the Bill which I had the honour to introduce on your behalf at the beginning of this Session.

Although not a victory, it is the next thing to one; every person that I have spoken to concurs in this opinion; and all seem to be convinced that zeal, judgment, and perseverance, among the operative classes, cannot fail of eventual and speedy success. Consider the vast superiority you enjoyed in the debate, and the complexion of the minority; I neither speak nor think with disrespect of the parties who opposed us, but we are not exceeding the limits of propriety when we seek to derive consolation and encouragement from the moral and social authority of those who have given us their support.

It is become evident, from the language held by some of your opponents, that the fear of being obliged to expend more capital, and call a larger number of hands into employment, lies at the bottom of much of their resistance. The demand, nevertheless, is most just. The manufacturers summon the landed interest to improve the condition of their people by a more abundant and costly cultivation of the soil—I heartily concur with them: the agriculturalists reply by inviting the manufacturers to do the same for their workmen, in the erection of additional machinery, and a fairer distribution of labour.

Persevere, therefore, in the full sense of the justice of your cause.

I have never entertained at any time so strong an assurance as I do this day that we shall soon, by God's blessing, attain the object of our toils and hopes. I urge you, by every consideration of yourselves and of your children, to redouble your efforts; and so far as any human being can presume to anticipate futurity I may promise, on my part, an unyielding determination in the pursuit of this your great and undeniable right.

I am, Gentlemen,
Your sincere friend and servant,
ASHLEY

Lord Ashley to the Central Short Time Committees, 27 May 1846

The Ten Hours' Act was finally passed in June 1847, restricting women and young persons to a 63-hour week from July and to 58 hours from 1848. However, a small group of Lancashire employers discovered a loophole in the law and employed workers for brief periods through a 15-hour day. Reformers were bitterly divided over this new problem, but the varied groups united to bring a test case against David Mills, a sympathetic Heywood master. Horner's sub-inspector, T. D. Ryder, brought the action in October 1849, with Cobbett's son John (1800–77) as prosecutor. Mills agreed to a conviction, but on appeal to the Court of Exchequer the reformers were defeated, in February 1850. Despite bitter opposition from Oastler, Stephens, the Fieldens, and Ferrand, Ashley and his followers accepted the compromise Bill of Sir George Grey (1799–1882), which forbade relays but increased weekly hours to 60. It was passed in August.

48 RYDER v MILLS

Judgment delivered in the Court of Exchequer, Friday,
February 8th, 1850.
(*From Mr. Gurney's Shorthand Notes*).

Mr. Baron Parke—The question raised by this special case,
by the agreement between the Crown and the defendant, is,
whether it is an offence against the Factory Acts, or any of them,
to employ a young person in a factory for ten hours and no more
in one day, such ten hours ending at a period which is more than
ten hours from the time when another child or young person
first began to work in the morning of such day in such factory, if
such last-mentioned ten hours are counted consecutively from
that time, omitting only the meal times?

The question depends entirely on the proper construction to
be put on those Acts, and more particularly on the 7th Victoria,
cap. 15. These Acts must be construed according to the established rules for the construction of statutes. In a court of law we
have only to ascertain the meaning of the words used by the
Legislature, and when that is ascertained we have to carry it into
effect, and we are not to enquire whether the enactments are
dictated by sound policy or not; that question is exclusively for
the consideration of Parliament. We agree also with the Attorney
General that though the immediate question in this case did
relate to adult females, who are more capable of taking care of
themselves, and of continued labour, than children, and consequently need less protection, and on whom the restriction from
employing themselves as they may think best appears more of a
hardship, the point to be decided is the same as if we were considering the case of children and young persons only, for the
Legislature has clearly put all females on the same footing as they
are. Indeed, the case as agreed on by both parties states that to be
the question. Is, then, the owner of a factory liable to the penalty
in respect to the employment of a child or young person in the
manner stated?

. . . On the opening of the argument by the Attorney General,

we thought the defendant meant to contend that the time limited
by the 26th section of the 7th Victoria, cap. 15, was to be calculated for each child or young person from the time that such
child or young person first began to work in the morning; and
that argument seemed to us to be altogether untenable, as being
against the ordinary and grammatical sense of the words in that
section.

But such is not the construction contended for by the learned
counsel for the defendant. He admits, and properly, that it is
clearly the ordinary meaning of the words in that section, that
the period from which the time is to be reckoned for all children
and young persons working at the factory is that time when the
first child or young person that was employed therein began to
work. Both sides are agreed upon this limit of the time, and there
can be not the least doubt about it. So, also, it is perfectly clear
that the times for meals for all young persons must all be at the
same period of the day, according to the plain words of the 36th
section . . .

But it is contended for the defendant, that the other limit—the
end of the time of working for all children and young persons—
has not been prescribed, and that it has not been enacted that
the time for the cessation of labour for all should be that when
the first ceased labour. Certainly this has not been done in
express words and nothing was more easy than to have said, in
the 26th section, that the 12 hours—reduced to 11 and 10 by the
subsequent statute, the 10th Victoria, cap. 29—should end
when any one had worked that time; or to have said, in the 36th
section, that all young persons should have the time for labour
as well as for meals at the same period of the day.

We must, then, consider whether, in the absence of express
words to this effect, we can collect from other parts of the Act
that this was the meaning of the Legislature so clearly and unequivocally as to call upon us to give effect to it, and punish the
defendant.

Undoubtedly if there was such an enactment it would have
the effect of securing to the children and young persons, whom

it was most certainly the object of the Legislature to protect against their own improvidence, or that of their parents, the more effectual superintendence and care of the inspectors. Without question it would more effectually prevent them from being overworked, and secure to them more completely the benefit of some education in public schools which the Legislature meant them to enjoy; it would advance the intended remedy. But then this result could only have been obtained by a larger sacrifice of the interest of the owners of factories, and we cannot assume that Parliament would disregard so important a consideration.

At any rate, a court of justice cannot render a man liable to a penalty merely because it might think that it would better promote the supposed object of the Legislature than the provisions of the statue according to their ordinary construction.

The words used must plainly and clearly show that the act complained of is punishable . . .

The ground upon which we proceed is, that though the Act of Parliament (taken in conjunction with the 10th Victoria, cap. 29) does distinctly forbid the employment of young persons, and therefore all females, for more than ten hours, and those to be taken between half-past 5 in the morning and half-past eight at night; though it distinctly requires that the time of all is to begin to be computed from the beginning of the first to work, and that an hour and a half shall be allowed for meals, and for all at the same time, it has not imposed in sufficiently clear terms any other restriction on the employment of young persons, and they are therefore at liberty to agree together for working for less than the whole of that time within the limits before-mentioned, ending at half-past eight, or any previous time that they please, and with any intervals of leisure that may be thought convenient.
The Champion, 9 March 1850

PART THREE

The Factory System and Society

Byy the mid-century the factory system was secure, and the domestic system was in full retreat in the greater industries. The manufacturer-dominated Anti-Corn Law League had been largely satisfied by the repeal of the Corn Laws in 1846. What John Bright had described as 'a movement of the commercial and industrial classes against the Lords and the great proprietors of the soil' naturally welcomed the first blow against 'the Barons', seeing it as an assertion of industry's rights in the new society. After the hungry years of the early 1840s and the virtual collapse of Chartism in 1848 a number of moderate liberal trade unions developed, particularly among the skilled craftsmen. Britain entered the second half of the century as the Workshop of the World, parading its new confidence at the Great Exhibition of 1851—a wondrous achievement to a generation fascinated by the abilities and capabilities of its industrial classes.

The Masters' Case Sadler's Bill and investigation provoked many protests from employers. Masters in each textile industry denied the allegations brought against them, agreed that abuses occurred elsewhere, claimed that work was healthy and light, insisted that child labour was essential to the economy of both the family and the factory, and generally supported *laisser-faire*. In the following extracts Joseph Birley (1782–1847), the greatest Manchester cotton manufacturer; an anonymous employer;

and Vernon Royle, another Manchester master, explain their attitudes.

——————

49 Every station in life has, more or less, its abuses—and workers in Cotton Factories are not exempt. Isolated cases, some true, some coloured, some entirely false, some of old date, are no proof of general suffering. It neither is the practice nor can be the interest of the owners of Factories to enervate or otherwise injure the persons whom they employ—on the contrary, it is necessary that they be alert and attentive; for attention, and not hard labour, is their constant duty ... Tales of sorrow, got up for a Parliamentary Committee, cannot establish the justness of a sweeping accusation.

... If [the master manufacturers] be villified and fettered as ignorant meddling enthusiasts and philanthropists are now attempting, but not at their own expense, establishments for spinning and weaving will still flourish,—but not in Great Britain. Joseph Birley. *Sadler's Bill. Cotton Branch*, 6, 7. Manchester, 1832

50 ... I believe that you have been imposed upon by the exaggerations and misstatements of parties who conceive it is their interest to procure the passing of the bill, and that your fears and imagination have been more than ordinarily excited ...

... The silk, worsted, and woollen mills are the most healthy, and the flax and tow, and cotton, the most unhealthy ... [but] the factory is, to many of its inmates, frequently a palace, in point of everything which contributes to salubrity ... the reflection and thought necessary in the management of its occupations, improves the faculties and intellect of the population, to an extent which renders it the most intelligent mass, in the same station of life, which is to be found in the world ...

The first and immediate consequence of limiting the ages of children employed, to "under 9 years" will be to throw out of employment all that class of hands. This is perhaps the most

cruel stroke to the poor man which could have been inflicted . . .
this threatened invasion of the rights of the parent over the child
[is] an infringement of the liberty of the subject, and a direct
violation of the homes of Englishmen . . . The bill is, in fact, a
reversion to the rude and barbarous legislation of Lycurgus . . .
[it] "out-Herods Herod" . . . [and] saddles the British operative
with an idle, unprofitable family, till they be nine years' old.

. . . The prostitution of this vaunted "measure of humanity" to
selfish and sinister purposes, is not an imaginary or conjectural
degradation. It is disgustingly notorious . . . the quantum of
goods produced in mills and factories will be diminished in direct
proportion to the curtailment of the hours of labour. *A Letter to
Sir John Cam Hobhouse, Bart., M.P. on "The Factories Bill", By A
Manufacturer*, 6, 11, 13–14, 16, 18, 35, 38. 1882

51 . . . We contend that the man of property, the Capitalist,
who devotes all his time, who applies all his energies to increase
his wealth, by building mills and factories, and so employing the
poor, is the greatest benefactor the poor man can have . . .

. . . The old and the young are essentially necessary to each
other, and form a whole, and make a full and beneficial division
of labour: to say, therefore, to the young, you shall work ten
hours a day, and to the old, or all above eighteen or twenty-one
years of age, you may work as many hours as you please, would
be just the same as if you said to a bricklayer, you Mr. Bricklayer,
may work as many hours as you please, but your labourer shall
give over work at four o'clock in the afternoon.

. . . One can hardly believe that men can be found so visionary
as to believe that an Act of Parliament can regulate the hours of
labour, can create food and a demand for labour.

. . . The ten hours bill . . . will be a bill to impoverish the poor
and cover the land with wretchedness. Factory time bill makers
are mockers of the poor and the needy, there is poison in the alms
of their charity. Vernon Royle. *The Factory System defended, in reply
to some parts of the Speech of G. Condy, Esq.*, . . . 5, 23–4, 30–1, 37.
Manchester, 1833

In 1787 Samuel Greg (1758–1834), the son of a Belfast ship-
owner, established his famous factory community at Styal in
Cheshire. His sons, Robert Hyde (1795–1875), Samuel (1804–
75), and William Rathbone (1809–81) had varied careers. In
1831 William—later a Commissioner of Customs, Comptroller
of the Stationery Office, and liberal-humanist author—anonymously published an *Enquiry into the State of the Manufacturing
Population*, which strongly condemned industrial conditions.
Robert, economist, antiquary, industrialist, and Liberal MP for
Manchester in 1839–41, was a strong opponent of factory legislation and condemned William's pamphlet as '*little more than a
college thesis*, written before he had any experience and scarcely
any acquaintance with factories'. The following extracts ade-
quately indicate Robert's views as a Liberal manufacturer in
1837.

---

52   . . . In defiance of justice, and, we should think, of strict
parliamentary usage, Mr. Sadler immediately published the
evidence, and gave to the world such a mass of ex-parte statements and of gross falsehoods and calumnies, as they are now
generally admitted to be, as probably never found their way into
any public document.

. . . It is much in favour of the Mill-owners' case that they have
at all times courted enquiry and challenged investigation . . .

[The] facts, resting as they do upon general and unquestion-
able data, show how much the public mind has been abused,
respecting the extent and amount of the evils resulting from
Factory employment. The *evils*, such as they have been, *have no
necessary connection with factory labour*, and the circumstance that
we are anxious, most emphatically, to press upon our reader's
attention, is, that *they did not arise under the present law, but when there
was no law, and when children might enter the mills at any age, and work
any number of hours, and when, in fact, they did work 72 hours, in the
best regulated mills*.

What evils can possibly be apprehended now, under a law
scrupulously enforced . . .?

. . . The evidence given before Mr. Sadler's Committee is *radically defective*, for it contains the statements *of one side only*, that against the factories and the masters . . . the evidence, such as it is, *was not given on oath* . . . [it] has every vice which can attach to evidence.

. . . The soundness of [Fielden's] judgment may still further be impeached as the advocate for a *legislative interference with wages, and the establishment of a board, for the regulation of them* . . . [He] can scarcely have heard of the name of Adam Smith . . .

It is proposed, then, by the "Short Time Committee", and Lord Ashley and his party, *to limit the productive energy of the . . . great staple manufacturers, including steam-engines, machinery, and grown-up men,* to NINE HOURS AND A HALF DAILY.

Such is the proposal which, strange to say, is heard without alarm by the Government, the monied interest, and the corn monopolists; with apathy by those whose property is at stake, and with approbation by a great political party, and by a humane but ignorant public . . .

Our only advantages consist in cheap machinery and low rate of interest. By restricting our mills to 69 hours a week, we have given up these advantages; by restricting them to 58, we not only annihilate them, but *hand them over to the enemy* . . .

. . . In case of a "Ten Hours Bill" being passed, the actual migration of English mill-owners, machinery, and capital will *hasten the period, already approaching with certainty,* when the markets of Europe and America will be closed, and when our customers will become our rivals.

. . . The simple circumstance of so large a proportion of the produce of our mills being exported, renders all discussion of the WISDOM of a "Ten Hours Bill" . . . entirely needless . . .

Another Time Book has been introduced by the Inspectors, in which the mill-owner enters, not at what periods daily, every child *actually comes into and goes out of the mill, but at what moment of time, every child shall make its entries and exits for the next twelve months.* The mill-owner, therefore, guarantees matters over which he has little or no control, and thereby puts himself at the mercy, not merely of the Inspector and his Superintendent, but of every servant, or even common spy. Who would not shrink from such a responsibility? . . . Neither are the fear and danger of prosecution, by any means visionary.

. . . It is much to be regretted that the present Factory Law, and the regulations of the Inspectors, tend to *destroy all good feeling, and to aggravate misunderstandings where they exist*. The Inspector's regulations are founded upon the principle of the master being *a tyrant and a cheat*; and that the operatives must look to the *Inspector*, rather than to *him*, for justice and protection . . .

We are sorry to see on the part of one of the Inspectors a call for *farther powers*, for authority to the Superintendent to enter the mills without the consent of the owner . . . To give to the Superintendent an absolute right of entrance into the mills, would be extremely offensive to the proprietors, and probably defeat some of the most important objects of the bill . . . if granted, hostility will be commenced, and all hopes of the Relay system, and any good arising from the bill, to balance its evil, will be gone for ever. The children will remain without food as well as education, the operatives will be extremely distressed, and the prosperity of the manufacturers seriously compromised . . .

. . . Now, the Inspector [Horner] should remember that the unfortunate mill-owner is allowed *neither jury, nor a power of appeal*, however unjust he may consider his sentence to be. The humanity and equity of the magistrate, alone, stands between him and his prosecutor. How can the Inspector desire that this discretion, *universally and properly granted to judges*, should be taken away, or limited, in order that the extravagant powers of himself and his superintendents may be increased?

Besides, does the Inspector suppose that it is no punishment to a *man*, we will say nothing of a *gentleman of education and standing in society* equal to himself, to be dragged into a court of justice, tried and condemned, and to have his name entered on a register of convicts? But this appears to be entirely overlooked, and the magistrates are reprimanded because they impose a penalty of £2 instead of £10. R. H. Greg. *The Factory Question, considered in*

K

*relation to its effects on the health and morals of those employed in factories,
And the "Ten Hours Bill" in relation to its effects upon the Manufacturers
of England, and those of Foreign Countries . . .,* 7–8, 28–9, 63–5, 68–9,
74–5, 89, 121, 123–5, 127, 129–30, 131–5. 1837

The 'Intellectual' Attitude   Academic writers largely agreed
with the views of the Liberal masters, accepting and propagating
the tenets of *laisser-faire*, free trade, and 'classical' political
economy. While this liberalism envisaged a free society, un-
hampered by ill-considered Government intervention, it often
offered a bleak solution to working-class problems. At Oxford in
the Easter term of 1830 Nassau Senior expounded an 'iron law of
wages', later publishing his lectures to demonstrate to rioting
agricultural workers that a fixed 'wages fund' precluded any
wage increase by State or trade union action; in Glasgow and
London Andrew Ure denounced any criticism of industrial employers; from Cambridge Charles Babbage [see p 24] wrote
admiringly of 'the triumphs and achievements' of science and
industry; and in 1837 Senior (1790–1864), turned his attention
to factory legislation. Professor of Political Economy at Oxford
in 1825–30 and 1847–52 and Master in Chancery from 1836 to
1855, he was the leading academic apostle of economic liberalism
in the 1830s. A Malthusian, he favoured abolition of the Poor
Law and considerably influenced the Royal Commission's
Report of 1834. Inevitably, he opposed factory legislation. With
others of his kind, he accepted the views of Edmund and Henry
Ashworth, the Bolton Quakers, whose mills and methods seemed
ideal to liberal visitors and hateful for workers and reformers.
Senior's most famous thesis was that profit was made only in the
last hour of a 12-hour day. Such Lancashire Tory masters as
William Kenworthy (1804–56) of Blackburn and Robert Gardner of Preston showed in the 1840s that shorter hours actually
increased productivity; but Senior was widely followed.

53   Mr. Horner agrees with me in thinking that a reduction of
the hours of work in cotton factories, to ten hours a day, would

be attended by the most fatal consequences, and that the evil would fall first on the working classes . . . He agrees with me as to the hostility of the working classes to the present measure, and as to their hope, by making it intolerable, to pave the way to a ten-hours' bill; and on the necessity of destroying this hope, and the mischief which it produces, by a strong expression on the part of the legislature, of a determination not to interfere further with the labour of those who are past childhood . . . These are important admissions, and prove not only the absurdity of imposing any additional restrictions on the cotton trade, but the necessity, if we wish to render the Factory Act useful, or even tolerable, of amending some of its existing enactments.

. . . Scarcely any manufacturer knows what are his neighbour's profits, or can tell accurately what are his own . . . I fully concur with Mr. Horner in believing the relay system to be the best mode of reconciling the education of the children with the productive use of the fixed capital employed . . .

We have now been for some time in the centre of the cotton district. Our principal objects of inquiry have been the effects of the Factory Regulation Act, as respects the cotton manufacture, and the consequences which may be expected from further legislative inference. And as Lord Ashley's motion is at hand, and will probably be disposed of before our return, I think you may not be unwilling to hear the results to which we have as yet come; although in stating them, I have no doubt that I shall say much with which you are familiar.

I have always been struck by the difference between the hours of work usual over the whole world in cotton factories and in other employments; and did not, until now, perceive the reasons. It seems to arise from two causes: first, the great proportion of fixed to circulating capital, which makes long hours of work desirable; and, secondly, the extraordinary lightness of the labour, if labour it can be called, which renders them practicable. I will take them separately:

1. I find the usual computation to be that the fixed capital is in the proportion of four to one to the circulating; so that if a manu-

facturer has £50,000 to employ, he will expend £40,000 in erecting his mill, and filling it with machinery, and devote only £10,000 to the purchase of raw material (cotton, flour, and coals) and the payment of wages. I find also that the whole capital is supposed in general to be turned over (or, in other words, that goods are produced and sold representing the value of the whole capital, together with the manufacturer's profit) in about a year; in favourable times in rather less—in others, such as the present, in rather more. I find also that the net profit annually derived may be estimated at ten per cent., some computations placing it as low as seven and a half, others as high as eleven; ten I believe to be about the average. But in order to realize this net profit, a gross profit of rather more than fifteen per cent, is necessary; for although the circulating capital, being continually restored to its original form of money, may be considered as indestructible, the fixed capital is subject to incessant deterioration, not only from wear and tear, but also from constant mechanical improvements, which in eight or nine years render obsolete, machinery which when first used was the best of its kind.

Under the present law, no mill in which persons under eighteen years of age are employed (and, therefore, scarcely any mill at all) can be worked more than eleven and a half hours a-day, that is, twelve hours for five days in the week and nine on Saturday.

Now, the following analysis will show that in a mill so worked, the whole net profit is derived *from the last hour*. I will suppose a manufacturer to invest £100,000: £80,000 in his mill and machinery, and £20,000 in raw material and wages. The annual return of that mill, supposing the capital to be turned once a-year and gross profits to be fifteen per cent., ought to be goods worth £115,000, produced by the constant conversion and reconversion of the £20,000 circulating capital, from money into goods and from goods into money, in periods of rather more than two months. Of this £115,000 each of the twenty-three half hours of work produces 5-115ths, or one twenty-third. Of these

23-23ds, (constituting the whole £115,000) twenty, that is to say, £100,000 out of the £115,000, simply replace the capital— one twenty-third (or £5,000 out of the £115,000), makes up for the deterioration of the mill and machinery. The remaining 2-23ds, that is, the last two of the twenty-three half hours of every day, produce the net profit of ten per cent. If, therefore (prices remaining the same), the factory could be kept at work thirteen hours instead of eleven and a half, by an addition of about £2,600 to the circulating capital, the net profit would be more than doubled. On the other hand, if the hours of working were reduced by one hour per day (prices remaining the same), net profit would be destroyed—if they were reduced by an hour and a half, even *gross* profit would be destroyed . . .

. . . "When a labourer", said Mr. Ashworth to me, "lays down his spade, he renders useless, for that period, a capital worth eighteen pence. When one of our people leaves the mill, he renders useless a capital that has cost £100".

2. The exceeding easiness of cotton-factory labour renders long hours of work *practicable*. With the exception of the mule spinners, a very small proportion of the operatives, probably not exceeding 12 or 15,000 in the whole Kingdom, and constantly diminishing in number, the work is merely that of watching the machinery, and piecing the threads that break . . . The work, in fact, is scarcely equal to that of a shopman behind a counter in a frequented shop—mere confinement, attention, and attendance.

Under these circumstances, cotton factories have always been worked for very long hours. From thirteen to fifteen, or even sixteen hours, appear to be the usual hours per day abroad. Our own, at their commencement, were kept going the whole twenty-four hours. The difficulty of cleaning and repairing the machinery, and the divided responsibility—arising from the necessity of employing a double staff of overlookers, bookkeepers, etc. have nearly put an end to this practice; but until Hobhouse's Act reduced them to sixty-nine, our factories generally worked from seventy to eighty hours per week. Any plan, therefore, which should reduce the present comparatively short hours, must either destroy profit, or reduce wages to the Irish standard, or raise the price of the commodity, by an amount which it is not easy for me to estimate.

The estimate in the paper, signed by the principal fine spinners, is, that it would raise prices by 16 per cent. That the increase of price would be such as to occasion, even in the home market, a great diminution of consumption, I have no doubt; and from all that I read and hear, on the subject of foreign competition, I believe that it would, in a great measure, exclude us from the foreign market, which now takes off three-fourths of our annual production.

It must never be forgotten, that in manufactures, with every increase of the quantity produced, the relative expense of production is diminished—and, which is the same thing, that with every diminution of production, the relative expense of production is increased . . . And this general law applies more and more forcibly, in proportion as the manufacture in question employs more expensive machinery and a greater division of labour: to the cotton manufacture, therefore, beyond all others. Up to the present time, production and cheapness have increased together. The yarn that cost forty shillings a pound when we consumed only 10,000,000 of pounds of cotton, now, when we consume 280,000,000, costs two shillings. Increase of price, and diminution of consumption, will therefore act and react on one another. Every increase of price will further diminish consumption; and every further diminution of consumption will occasion an increased relative cost of production, and consequently a further increase of price. First will go the foreign market—already in a precarious state, and, once lost, irrecoverable; since, according to the law to which I have referred, the more our rivals produce, —the wider the markets which are opened to their competition, in consequence of the rise of English prices—the cheaper they will be able to produce. This again, by diminishing the quantity produced at home, will increase its relative cost of production; and that again will increase prices, and diminish consumption;

—until I think I see, as in a map, the succession of causes which may render the cotton manufactures of England mere matter of history.

I have no doubt, therefore, that a ten hours' bill would be utterly ruinous. And I do not believe that any restriction whatever, of the present hours of work, could be safely made.

. . . The relay system appears on the whole, as far as this [the Manchester] district is concerned, to have failed. . . The usual plan is to employ one set of children for the first eight hours of the day, and to get on as well as may be during the remaining four without them . . .

It may easily be supposed that the *operatives* are outra geous against this state of things. Their original object was to raise the price of their *own* labour. For this purpose the spinners, who form . . . a very small (about 1-20th) but a powerful body among them, finding that they could not obtain a limitation of the hours of work to ten by combination, tried to affect it through the legislature. They knew that Parliament would not legislate for adults. They got up therefore a frightful, and (as far as we have heard and seen) an utterly unfounded picture of the ill-treatment of the children, in the hope that the legislature would restrain all persons under 18 years old to ten hours, which they knew would, in fact, restrict the labour of adults to the same period. The Act having not only defeated this attempt, but absolutely turned it against them,—having, in fact, increased their labour and diminished their pay,—they are far more vehement for a ten hours' bill than before, and are endeavouring by every means to impede the working of the existing Act, and to render its enactments vexatious or nugatory. We hear everywhere of their conspiring to entrap the masters into penalties, by keeping the children too long in the mill, by keeping them from school, and by all the petty annonyances by which trouble can be created.

. . . The manufacturer is tired of regulations—what he asks is tranquility—*implora pace* . . .

. . . The factory work-people in the country districts are the plumpest, best clothed, and healthiest looking persons of the labouring class that I have ever seen. The girls, especially, are far more good-looking (and good looks are fair evidence of health and spirits) than the daughters of agricultural labourers. The wages earned per family are more than double those of the South.

. . . The difference in appearance when you come to the Manchester operatives is striking; they are sallow and thinner. But when I went through their habitations in Irish Town, and Ancoats, and Little Ireland, my only wonder was that tolerable health could be maintained by the inmates of such houses. These towns, for such they are in extent and population, have been erected by small speculators with an utter disregard to every thing except immediate profit. A carpenter and a bricklayer club together to buy a patch of ground, and cover it with what they call houses . . .

I must own that I am somewhat alarmed at the rumours that the Government propose to render the Factory Act more stringent, in compliance with Mr. Horner's requisitions . . . [and] would . . . leave the enforcement of the Act to the clergy and country gentlemen,—classes generally opposed to the mill-owners in habits and politics, and without practical knowledge of the system in the working of which they would have to interfere . . . To enforce ventilation and drainage, and give means and motives to education, seems to me all that can be done by positive enactment. Nassau W. Senior. *Letters on the Factory Act, As it affects the Cotton Manufacture, Addressed To The Right Honourable the President of the Board of Trade* . . ., 3–5, 6, 11–13, 14–16, 17, 18, 19–20, 22, 23, 24, 26, 29. 1837

Many masters bitterly resented the attacks made by reformers from the Right and the Left. The general counterattack assailed the Right as feudal and reactionary and the Left as either violent or dishonest. Andrew Ure (1778–1857), the employers' apologist, presents a typical argument in the following extract.

54 The ancient feeling of contempt entertained by the country gentlemen towards the burghers, which vented itself during the lawless period of the middle ages, in every form of contumely and outrage, seems still to rankle in the breasts of many members of our aristocracy, is still fostered by the panegyrists of their order, and displayed itself, not equivocally, in the late parliamentary crusade against the factories. One of their most eloquent advocates and partisans speaks of the great development of our mechanical industry in the following scornful terms:—"It is a wen, a fungous excrescence from the body politic; the growth might have been checked, if the consequences had been apprehended in time; but now it has acquired so great a bulk, its nerves have branched so widely, and the vessels of the tumour are so inosculated into some of the principal veins and arteries of the natural system, that to remove it by absorption is impossible, and excision will be fatal".*

Could a metaphor have proved anything, a more appropriate one might have been found, in the process of vegetable and animal generation, to illustrate the great truth, that Providence has assigned to man the glorious function of vastly improving the productions of nature by judicious culture, and of working them up into objects of comfort and elegance with the least possible expenditure of human labour—an undeniable position which forms the basis of our Factory System . . .

It has, however, been the fate of this *polytechnic*, as of the best philanthropic dispensation ever made to man, to be misrepresented and reviled, not only by strangers ignorant of its intrinsic excellence, but by the very objects of its bounty, the children of its care. When the wandering savage becomes a citizen, he renounces many of his dangerous pleasures in return for tranquillity and protection. He can no longer gratify at his will a revengeful spirit upon his foes, nor seize with violence a neighbour's possessions. In like manner, when the handicraftsman exchanges hard work with fluctuating employment and pay, for continuous labour of a lighter kind with steady wages, he must necessarily renounce his old prerogative of stopping when he

* Southey's Colloquies, vol. i, p. 171.

pleases, because he would thereby throw the whole establish-ment into disorder. Of the amount of the injury resulting from the violation of the rules of automatic labour he can hardly ever be a proper judge; just as mankind at large can never fully esti-mate the evils consequent upon an infraction of God's moral law. Yet the factory operative, little versant in the great operations of political economy, currency, and trade, and actuated too often by an invidious feeling towards the capitalist who animates his otherwise torpid talents, is easily persuaded by artful dema-gogues, that his sacrifice of time and skill is beyond the portion of his recompense, or that fewer hours of industry would be an ample equivalent for his wages. This notion seems to have taken an early and inveterate hold of the factory mind, and to have been riveted from time to time by the leaders of those secret combinations, so readily formed among a peculiar class of men, concentrated in masses within a narrow range of country.

Instead of repining as they have done at the prosperity of their employers, and concerting odious measures to blast it, they should, on every principle of gratitude and self-interest, have rejoiced at the success resulting from their labours, and by regularity and skill have recommended themselves to monied men desirous of engaging in a profitable concern, and of procur-ing qualified hands to conduct it. Thus good workmen would have advanced their condition to that of overlookers, managers, and partners in new mills, and have increased at the same time the demand for their companions' labour in the market. It is only by an undisturbed progression of this kind that the rate of wages can be permanently raised or upheld. Had it not been for the violent collisions and interruptions resulting from erroneous views among the operatives, the factory system would have been developed still more rapidly and beneficially for all concerned than it has been, and would have exhibited still more frequently gratifying examples of skilful workmen becoming opulent pro-prietors. Every misunderstanding either repels capital altogether, or diverts it from flowing, for a time, in the channels of a trade liable to strikes.

It is therefore deeply to be deplored, for the sake of all parties, as well as for our country's welfare, that the cotton-spinners in particular have been so blinded by prejudice and passion, as never rightly to comprehend the force of this elementary principle. Had their conduct been governed by it, they would have had better wages, and might have appropriated to their own use the whole amount of their earnings, instead of squandering no inconsiderable portion of them upon the fomenters of misrule— the functionaries of their unions. The means which they have all along enjoyed for maintaining themselves and families in comfort have been, generally speaking, better than those possessed in other parts of the kingdom by the average of those artisans who have expensive tools to provide, and tedious apprenticeships to serve; for the net wages of a cotton-spinner have been rarely under 30s. a week all the year round, nay, sometimes considerably more; constituting an income nearly three times as great as that of the farm-labourer or hand-weaver for as many hours' occupation, and for much severer toil.

. . . . When they choose to strike they can readily join in the blow, and by stopping they suffer merely the loss of wages for the time, while they occasion to their master loss of interest on his sunk capital, his rent, and his taxes, as well as injury to the delicate moving parts of metallic mechanisms by inaction in our humid climate . . .

If it be a maxim of equity in every state that false accusation should recoil on the heads of its authors, what punishment ought to be rewarded to those who, after committing unknown severities upon their dependent children, should magnify the extent of the evil a thousandfold, and lay all this load of exaggerated crime on persons not only entirely innocent and unconscious of its existence, but avowed enemies to its commission in any degree.

The following short extract of evidence given on oath by respectable witnesses will confirm the preceding statement. "Who is it that beats the children? The spinner". "Not the master?—No; the masters have nothing to do with the children

—they don't employ them". "Do you (a spinner) pay and employ
your own piecers?—Yes; it is the general rule in Manchester;
but our master is very strict over us, that we don't employ them
under age". "Are the children ever beaten?—Sometimes they get
beat, but not severely; for sometimes they make the stuff to
waste, and then correction is needful; but that is unknown to the
master—he does not allow beating at all".

No master would wish to have any wayward children to work
within the walls of his factory, who do not mind their business
without beating, and he therefore usually fines or turns away any
spinners who are known to maltreat their assistants. Hence, ill-
usage of any kind is a very rare occurrence. I have visited many
factories, both in Manchester and in the surrounding districts,
during a period of several months, entering the spinning rooms,
unexpectedly, and often alone, at different times of the day, and
I never saw a single instance of corporal chastisement inflicted
on a child, nor indeed did I ever see children in ill-humour. They
seemed to be always cheerful and alert, taking pleasure in the
light play of their muscles,—enjoying the mobility natural to
their age. The scene of industry, so far from exciting sad emotions
in my mind, was always exhilarating. It was delightful to observe
the nimbleness with which they pieced the broken ends, as the
mule carriage began to recede from the fixed roller-beam, and to
see them at leisure, after a few seconds' exercise of their tiny
fingers, to amuse themselves in any attitude they chose, till the
stretch and winding-on were once more completed. The work of
these lively elves seemed to resemble a sport, in which habit gave
them a pleasing dexterity. Conscious of their skill, they were
delighted to show it off to any stranger. As to exhaustion by the
day's work, they evinced no trace of it on emerging from the
mill in the evening; for they immediately began to skip about
any neighbouring play-ground, and to commence their little
amusements with the same alacrity as boys issuing from a school.
It is moreover my firm conviction, that if children are not ill-
used by bad parents or guardians, but receive in food and raiment the full benefit of what they earn, they would thrive better

when employed in our modern factories, than if left at home in apartments too often ill-aired, damp, and cold. Andrew Ure. *The Philosophy of Manufactures*, 277–81, 300–1. 1835

_____

Francis Place (1771–1854), the son of a prison bailiff, opened his tailor's shop in Charing Cross Road in 1799 and became a leader of London liberal Radicals. In 1824, with the Radical MP Joseph Hume (1777–1855), he organised the repeal of the Combination Acts against trade unions, and in 1831–2 he led an agitation for the Reform Bill. Place fully accepted liberal theory, however: trade unions were 'very mischievous associations'; Owen's theories were 'nonsensical doctrines'; and the Ten Hours agitation, as he told the reformers' Lancashire secretary, James Turner, in the following letter published in Roebuck's journal, was 'absurd'.

_____

55   ... You all know that the little master and the new master are the first to take advantage of the poverty of a workman, or his want of employment ...

... leave off railing at others, and go seriously to work for yourselves. 'God helps those who help themselves', says the proverb; and you may depend upon it that you will never be helped by any but yourselves ... Your proposed remedy of a short time-bill, is even more than absurd. It never will be granted. It ought not to be granted. No Parliament will ever pass a bill to prevent any class of manufacturers from carrying on their business in any manner they may think most advantageous, save only so far as relates to the employment of children; and a short-time bill is not necessary for their protection. A short-time bill would make the condition of the "factory workers" beyond all that they have hitherto endured, miserable indeed ...

I have never seen the inside of a cotton factory. It is almost certain that I shall never see the inside of one. I have read all the evidence taken by Committees of Parliament; I have read books and pamphlets; I have conversed with numbers of cottoners, masters as well as men; I understand much of the machinery used in all sorts of mills, and should like to see it in use. But I cannot voluntarily submit to seeing the misery of working it before my eyes. I abhor such scenes of degradation, as even the best of the cotton-mills cannot be free from. This will be treated as a ridiculous feeling, as an absurd prejudice; but to me, to whom human beings are valuable as they are intellectual and free, a cotton-mill is more abhorrent than I can find words with which to describe it! Francis Place. 'Handloom Weavers and Factory Workers, a Letter to James Turner, cotton spinner', 29 September 1835, *Pamphlets for the People*, I, 16 (nd)

Graham's Factory Bill of 1843 [see p 133] and its educational provisions strengthened the long-standing alliance between the textile manufacturers and the dissenting churches. The Anglican voluntary provision of schools vastly surpassed the Nonconformists' contribution, and some Nonconformists preferred the factory children to have no education rather than Anglican teaching. Various (and sometimes contradictory) arguments were raised; Edward Baines (1800–90), a Congregationalist and publicist of the Yorkshire Liberal employers, used most of them in a series of pamphlets. Here he deploys popular beliefs against both a Church of England 'infected' by the Oxford Movement and agricultural conditions.

56 My Lord,—If ever there was an occasion on which the Dissenters and Methodists throughout the Kingdom felt as one man, and on which their feelings of indignation, springing out of the deep conviction of their judgment, were strong and unconquerable, it was when they discovered the true character of Sir James Graham's Bill for establishing a *Compulsory Church* Education at the public expense . . .

. . . the cause of religious Liberty is now, and will long continue to be, in the most serious danger. There is at the bottom of this attack a spirit of High Church bigotry, fostered by clergymen whose ambition is as intense and insatiable as it is deep and crafty; and from that spirit—patient, vigilant, adroit, and trained in the very school of the Jesuits—we have everything to fear . . .

BUT the danger of the present times is exceedingly aggravated by a combination of circumstances that appears fortuitous. Attempts have been made with great perseverance for some years past to *blacken the manufacturing districts in the eyes of Parliament and of the public*. Political conflicts to which I need not allude have furnished the motives to those attempts. Some men, influenced by undoubted humanity, such as LORD ASHLEY, have been instruments to the same end. Commissions of inquiry have been appointed to bring to light all the abuses and evils existing in the manufacturing and mining districts (*not* in the agricultural) and they have succeeded, as they would have done in any other part of the known world, in producing full budgets and painting very dark pictures. And, lastly, the sudden and momentary turn-out of last August, though the most harmless movement on record, though provoked by severe distress, and though an experiment at the folly of which the workmen themselves laughed as soon as it was over, has been excessively magnified, so as to give the impression that the manufacturing districts are placed over a volcano ever ready to burst!

. . . My Lord, I engage to prove that the impression of alarm with respect to the state of the manufacturing districts, on which the authors of this Bill rely for success, is *absurdly false and injurious* . . . Let it be observed, I do not charge LORD ASHLEY or the Children's Employment Commission with *intentional* misrepresentation. But I do say that the *impression* likely to be produced by his speeches and their Report is *one-sided, exaggerated*, and *erroneous* in the extreme . . .

. . . Of course we cannot expect that in this poor, provincial, manufacturing, dissenting town of Leeds, there should be any thing like the *same amount* of *education*, or of *religion* as in the chosen abode of nearly all the Bishops and nearly all the Members of both Houses of Parliament. That would be extravagant. Let us expect nothing out of reason. Nevertheless, my Lord, I tell you, we have *more* of *both*! We have *more education*; we have *more religion*; and we have *less vice*! . . .

Now, my Lord, you can afford to abate a little of the pity you may have felt for poor Leeds. But, more, my Lord, much more than this—you will, I am sure, spare a little respect for that principle of *voluntary religious zeal* which has done *every thing* in Leeds, and will moreover pause before you adopt a *compulsory* measure *which might cut the sinew of that voluntary zeal.*

WOULD your Lordship have the goodness just to put these facts before SIR ROBERT INGLIS, and to hold him fast by the button till you are sure he has heard them? Would you ask him if he could give as good an account of Oxford? Would you also suggest to LORD ASHLEY and SIR JAMES GRAHAM to *look rather nearer home* . . .

. . . I MUST not conclude without saying, that if LORD ASHLEY will appoint a Commission to inquire into the state of the *Agricultural* population, he will find a sphere for his benevolent anxiety possessing at least as many claims upon him as the manufacturing towns. I believe, on the authority of the "Report of the Constabulary Force Commissioners", that the *majority* of the crimes attended with violence are now committed in the *rural* districts, although the population and property in towns have increased in a far more rapid proportion. I believe, on the evidence of the facts which induced your Lordship to propose the Bastardy clause of the New Poor Law, that the want of chastity in the rural districts is far more general than in the manufacturing districts. I believe, on the evidence of the wide-spread incendiarism and destruction of thrashing machines, that the lawlessness of the agricultural labourers, arising from their gross ignorance, is much more formidable than that of the manufacturing population. I believe, from such facts as the insurrection in favour of the imposter THOM in Kent, that the knowledge of religion is far less in the country than in towns. I am persuaded that there is no comparison between the manufacturing and agricultural labourers as to general intelligence, and habits of reading and thinking. It is beyond all question that the rate of

wages is much higher in manufactures than in agriculture,—that
the workmen employed in the former have better food, clothing,
and houses, and greater comforts than those employed in the
latter. Edward Baines. *The Manufacturing Districts Vindicated. A
Second Letter to the Right Honourable Lord Wharncliffe, Chairman of
Council on Education*, 1–3, 6–7, 10–11. Leeds, 1843

The Operation of Factory Legislation The working of the
Factory Acts inevitably depended to a large extent on the
vigilance and energy of the four Inspectors and their fifteen
Superintendents. In Scotland James Stuart appears to have been
lax, but the three other Inspectors—Leonard Horner, T. J.
Howell and R. J. Saunders—were hardworking men. The
following cases brought by Superintendent Robert Baker illustrate some of their difficulties. Until registration of births was
made compulsory in 1837, it was often hard to ascertain children's ages. Furthermore, as masters pointed out, the actual
employers of the children, with responsibility for discipline and
hours of work, were often the workers themselves.

57   IMPORTANT CONVICTION UNDER THE
                    FACTORY ACT

On Wednesday before the sitting magistrates at the Court
House, Bradford, Mr. Charles Craven, the parish clerk of Bradford, was charged by Mr. Baker, the superintendent of factories,
with falsifying a legal and correct certificate by writing upon the
margin after it had been signed by the curate. Mr. Baker stated
the case, and proved the identity of the certificate and the hand-
writing of the clerk, by the Rev. Mr. Butterfield. Mr. Craven at
once acknowledged that the writing was his, but said that he did
not know at the time that he was acting wrong, by writing upon
the margin, at the request of the mother, the time which she
stated to be the birth of the child. He did it rather as an act of
kindness to the parents than anything else; he had no benefit in
it or by it, and if he had known that there was wrong in doing so,
he would not have done it. He expressed his regret for having

L

done so, and threw himself on the clemency of the Bench. He was ordered to stand down, and the Bench consulted for a considerable time. On being again called up, the chairman addressed him in a feeling manner and pointed out the necessity of having faithful extracts made from the parish registers: that on a full consideration of the case, they were compelled by a sense of duty and justice to visit this offence severely. In this case there was no fine awarded by law; the punishment was imprisonment, and that for two months; but in consideration that it was a first offence, and was not committed for any interested motive, the sentence of the Bench was that he be imprisoned in the House of Correction at Wakefield for fourteen days. However, before the sessions broke up the defendant was again brought before the Bench and liberated on bail to appear when called upon within three months. *Leeds Intelligencer*, 24 March 1838

FACTORY INFORMATION

Yesterday, Mr. John Howard, carpet manufacturer, was summoned before the sitting magistrates, Dr. Williamson and James Musgrave, Esq., at the Court House, Leeds, charged by Mr. Superintendent Baker with having worked a boy under thirteen years of age more than nine hours a day. Mr. Howard acquitted himself of any liability in the matter, by showing that he had several times given orders for the Act to be strictly observed in his works, and left the execution of it to his workmen. The information was discharged as to Mr. Howard, but the slubber who employed the boy and who paid his wages and had power to discharge him was fined five shillings and costs. It appeared that the boy was sent to school for two hours every forenoon and that the working time was very little more than forty eight hours a week. *Leeds Intelligencer*, 15 December 1838

The Ten Hours Act provided new work for the Inspectorate, as young persons and women were now more tightly controlled than either children or adult males. The Inspectors tried to prevent the use of full or staggered relays of young people, but had varied support in the courts—not least because of the hostility of some magistrates. The two cases described below demonstrate the gathering confusion in the late 1840s over the meaning of the Act.

___

58 BREACH OF THE TEN HOURS FACTORY ACT
Last Monday several woollen manufacturers from Bramley appeared before the Mayor and D. Lupton, Esq., at the instance of Robert Baker, Esq., who had summoned them for breaches of the Factory Act. Mr. Joseph Haley was the first party called. Mr. Baker, who gave Mr. Haley credit for having conducted his mill with great propriety, said he was charged with having unlawfully employed in his factory a young person above thirteen and under eighteen years of age more than ten hours a day. The simple fact was that by the 26th section of the Factory Act it was enacted that the time of any such worker should be reckoned from the time at which any young person commenced work in the morning. In this case the precise time for commencing work, was fixed by notice in Mr. Haley's mill, viz., at half past five in the morning. The complaint was that he had worked his mill by two relays of such young persons, the time of work being from half past five in the morning to half past eight at night, one set being worked in the morning and the other in the afternoon. This the law prohibited, and the clause he had quoted was inserted for the purpose of preventing this practice of working such young persons upon the relay system. This was a similar case to those which had been decided in other parts of the country, and he wished to have a decision upon it here. Mr. Haley might employ men as long as he liked and young children under thirteen years of age might be employed in relays, the act so providing, but in the case of adolescent persons, above that age and under eighteen, the law clearly prohibited the working of them in relays as charged against Mr. Haley.

The Mayor and Mr. Lupton both thought the law as quoted by Mr. Baker a hardship upon the manufacturer, but as the enactment was clear they had no alternative but to convict. Perhaps Mr. Baker would be content to take one charge only. Mr. Baker at once consented to this, on condition of the costs being paid in the other cases, observing that he only wished for a decision in order to establish the principle.

. . . This decision is in accordance with others given in this part of the country, but the question is one on which considerable difference of opinion prevails . . .

. . . We find, however, that in Lancashire, a decision the very opposite has been given, as the annexed paragraph taken from the *Manchester Examiner* of Tuesday will show:—

'Important decision under the New Factory Act. Legality of relays. Messrs. Jones, Brothers, and Co., of Moseley Street in Manchester and also of Bedford, in the parish of Leigh, were summoned to appear before the Atherton petty sessions by David Jones, sub-inspector of factories in the Bolton district, upon two informations of working a female and also a young person for more than ten hours in one day . . . Mr. Ovens, barrister, . . . contended that Messrs. Jones had not violated the law, inasmuch as the Legislature never contemplated so stringent a construction being put upon the act as to prevent a system of relays. The Bench declared they were unanimously of opinion they could not convict the Messrs. Jones. The case was therefore dismissed'. *Leeds Mercury*, 10 June 1848

The enforcement of the educational provisions of the 1833 Act—disliked by masters, employees, and children alike—proved a difficult task for the Inspectors. Horner 'had to reject the school voucher of the fireman, the children having been schooled in the coal-hole', and Saunders' 1838 Report included the following dismal account by Baker of the standards of the early factory schools.

59 You are aware that factory schools are of many kinds, from the coal-hole of the engine-house to the highest grade of infant education. The engine-man, the slubber, the burler, the book-keeper, the overlooker, the wife of any one of these, the small shopkeeper, or the next-door neighbour, with six or seven small children on the floor and in her lap, are by turns found "teaching the young idea how to shoot" in and about their several places of occupation for the two hours required by the law . . . I do not think that, among the 500 mills under my superintendence in the West Riding of Yorkshire, I should be able to name a dozen schools where the education is systematically good . . . Some . . . certificates I beg to put in, in proof of the miserable incapacity of [teachers], only regretting that I am unable at the same time to give a fac-simile of the hand-writing . . .

"this to sertify that 1838 thomas Cordingley as atend martha insep school tow hours per day January 6" . . .

"The above Named Children has Been twelve Hours in this School after the Manner of Scollers in the past week—Mary Collins" . . .

"This his to Certify that Christina Walker Comes to my School one halfe of the week—Hannah Hargreaves".

"This is to Certify that Eliza Johnson and John Johnson have attended my School two hours each day for the last six days and have been teached by me". Reports on the Effects of the Educational Provisions of the Factories Act, *Parliamentary Papers*, 1839, XLII, 412–13

_____

The Inspectors were increasingly involved in the problem of making machinery safe. Reformers had for long told stories of tired children falling into machines. Certainly, the regular speeding-up of the machines caused injury and sometimes death. Convinced by the evidence, Ashley campaigned for the fencing of dangerous machinery and a rudimentary form of workmen's compensation, from 1833 on. His Select Committee on the 1833 Act in 1841 demanded the covering of dangerous machinery and pulleys and the prohibition of machine-cleaning while the machine was working. The Inspectors generally supported him, and the 1844 Act prohibited the cleaning of working machines; ordered the fencing of machines, gearing, flywheels, engines and hoists; and provided a scale of fines and compensation. The following quotations demonstrate the reasons behind the Inspectors' concern and the method by which they sought to deal with the problem. They were not successful, and the question remained controversial.

60 On the 23rd November, Mary Ann Lees, aged 24, a married woman, the mother of one child, and in an advanced state of pregnancy, carried her husband's dinner to him, in a room in Messrs. T. & G. Marshall's mill (at Stockport) where he was employed as a dresser. She remained with him for a short time after the expiration of the dinner hour, and having inadvertently approached too near an upright shaft, revolving with considerable rapidity, her shawl was caught by it, and she was consequently dragged against the shaft, from which she was with much difficulty released after her left arm had been torn completely off above the elbow joint, so as to render amputation necessary . . . This accident, I think, affords another strong proof of the necessity for legislative interference, since it is obvious that some mill-owners will not take the precaution of fencing off dangerous machinery until compelled to do so by a stringent enactment. Report of Factory Inspector T. J. Howell, 31 December 1841, *Parliamentary Papers*, 1842, XXII, 430

61 FORM OF NOTICE to be given to the Occupier of a Factory, by an Inspector or Sub-Inspector, of such Part of the Machinery, or such Driving Strap or Band, in the Factory, as appears to him to be dangerous to the Workers.

To [*Name of Occupier*], Occupier of a [Description of the Manufacture] Factory, situated in the Parish of and County of

I hereby give you Notice, that the following Parts of the Machinery in your factory, namely [*here enumerate the Parts*], appear to me to be dangerous, and likely to cause bodily injury to the Workers employed in the Factory; and I am of opinion that they ought to be immediately well and securely fenced. And I hereby further give you Notice, that by the Act made in the ——Year of Her Majesty's Reign, intituled [*here set forth the Title of this Act*], it is provided, that if, after receiving this Notice, you shall neglect or fail to fence the above-enumerated Machinery, and if any Person shall suffer any bodily injury in consequence of such Neglect or Failure, you will be liable to a Penalty of One Hundred Pounds, over and above all Damages, Costs, and Charges to which you may be found liable in any Action brought against you by or on behalf of the Person so injured.

Given under my Hand, this   Day of   in the Year One thousand eight hundred and

(*Signed*)_____

Inspector [or Sub-Inspector]

Standard Notice on Dangerous Machinery, in 'An Act to Amend the Laws Relating to Labour in Factories', 7 & 8 Vic, c 15, 1844, Schedule D

Working-Class Organisations Trade clubs were widely established in the eighteenth century, and the woolcombers in particular had a large organisation, providing friendly society benefits and celebratory pageants on Bishop Blaize's Festival. A series of Acts, culminating in the Combination Acts of 1799 and 1800, banned trade unions, some of which, however, continued under the guise of friendly societies. Another old working-class tradition was also maintained—that of machine-wrecking. The reaction to new machines which threatened employment had often been to destroy them. During the Napoleonic wars such spontaneous outbursts gave way to organised action by machine-wrecking gangs. The Midland framework knitters in 1811 under a mysterious 'Ned Ludd' smashed frames making cheap goods; Yorkshire croppers, under George Mellor, smashed the gig-mills and shearing frames in 1812; and Lancashire and Cheshire weavers rioted against food prices and power looms. A wide use of spies and several hangings for machine-wrecking soon defeated the secret societies. A typical Luddite oath is given below.

---

62   I, A.B., of my own voluntary will, do declare and solemnly swear, that I never will reveal to any person or persons under the canopy of heaven, the names of the persons who compose this secret committee, their proceedings, meetings, places of abode; dress, features, complexion or anything else that might lead to a discovery of the same, either by word, deed, or sign, under the penalty of being sent out of the world by the first brother who shall meet me, and my name and character blotted out of existence, and never to be remembered but with contempt and abhorrence; and I further now do swear, that I will use my best endeavours to punish by death any traitor or traitors, should any rise up among us, whenever I can find him or them, and though he should fly to the verge of nature, I will pursue him with unceasing vengeance. So help me God and bless me to keep this my oath inviolable. Frank Peel. *The Risings of the Luddites, Chartists and Plugdrawers.* Heckmondwike, 1888

Perhaps the most militant textile unionists of the 1830s were the Glasgow cotton spinners. Well established and well organised, they fought hard against wage cuts and during an 1837 strike employed considerable violence. A murder charge and conviction for conspiracy helped to provoke a Parliamentary investigation of trade unionism. The following extract from the first (and only) report of the Select Committee is taken from the examination of Doherty on the history and attitudes of the Manchester spinners.

---

63   *Mr. Pringle.* Will you state generally for what purposes the combination took place?—There were several objects of the Spinners' association; the main object was to prevent reductions of wages; and next, if it be possible, and we hope it will be certain, to procure an Act of Parliament to lessen the hours of labour in factories. That point, I believe, in fact I know, during the whole of my connexion with the spinners of Manchester, has been one that has never changed. Our society has been abandoned at different periods, and our meetings given up, but we have never abandoned the hope and attempt to lessen the hours of labour by Act of Parliament.

Mr. O'Connell. You mean what is called the Ten Hours' Bill? —Yes; 10 hours or less.

Mr. Pringle. You do not deprecate the interference of the Legislature with such a subject as that?—No, we do not; we seek it.

To what extent, then, do you deprecate the interference of the Legislature with the interests of the workmen?—With regard to the mode of carrying on their combinations or anything of that description.

Are there any other objects or purpose for which you associate? —The other object of combination would be in endeavouring to prevent certain harsh treatment, to which we find we are gradually becoming more and more subjected.

Lord Ashley. You say that what is technically called the Factory Question has been the main object of your combination for many years?—It has for more than 20 years, to my knowledge; I can state as a fact, that in 1818, when our combination was broken up, in consequence of a strike that was unsuccessful, in the year or two following that, when the men contributed nothing to the funds of the union, they contributed regularly for the purpose of procuring an Act of Parliament upon that question, and one was enacted in 1819. First Report of the Select Committee on Combinations of Workmen, *Parliamentary Papers,* 1837–8, VIII, 256

———

In the hot summer of 1842, at a time of deep depression, there began a massive strike-wave in the industrial areas. The trouble spread to the textile factory districts when the Ashton masters announced a further wage reduction. Throughout August touring mobs drew the boiler plugs, thus closing the mills. Although at first doubtful about joining in, the Chartists eventually used the opportunity by carrying resolutions to stay out until the Charter was accepted; but they and such Conservatives as Graham and John Wilson Croker (1780–1857) suspected that the outbreak had been encouraged by Anti-Corn Law League employers, in order to embarrass a Protectionist Ministry. In the event, numerous arrests and sheer hunger drove the strikers back to work. In the following extracts Thomas Cooper (1805–92), the journalist leader of Leicester Chartism, describes the state of Manchester during the Chartist Convention of 1842; and Richard Pilling (b 1800), a weaver and father of nine children, who was blamed as 'the father of this great movement', explains the desperation of some operatives with starving families.

---

64 "The Plug Plot", of 1842, as it is still called in Lancashire, began in reductions of wages by the Anti-Corn-Law manufacturers, who did not conceal their purpose of driving the people to desperation, in order to paralyse the Government. The people advanced, at last, to a wild general strike, and pulled up the plugs so as to stop the works at the mills, and thus render labour impossible. Some wanted the men who spoke at the meetings held at the beginning of the strike to propose resolutions in favour of Corn Law Repeal; but they refused. The first meeting where the resolution was passed, "that all labour should cease until the People's Charter became the law of the land", was held on the 7th of August, on Mottram Moor. In the course of a week, the resolution had been passed in nearly all the great towns of Lancashire, and tens of thousands had held up their hands in favour of it ...

Samuel Bevinton was the strongest-minded man among the Chartists of the Potteries; and he said to me, "You had better get off to Manchester. You can do no more good here". I agreed that he was right ...

When I entered the railway carriage at Crewe, some who were going to the Convention recognised me,—and, among the rest, Campbell, secretary of the "National Charter Association". . . .

So soon as the City of Long Chimneys came in sight, and every chimney was beheld smokeless, Campbell's face changed, and with an oath he said, "Not a single mill at work! something must come out of this and something serious too!"

... In the streets, there were unmistakeable signs of alarm on the part of the authorities. Troops of cavalry were going up and down the principal thoroughfares, accompanied by pieces of artillery, drawn by horses. In the evening, we held a meeting in the Reverend Mr. Schofield's Chapel, where O'Connor, the Executive, and a considerable number of delegates were present; and it was agreed to open the Conference, or Convention, in form, the next morning, at nine o'clock. We met at that hour, the next morning, Wednesday, the 17th of August, when James Arthur of Carlisle was elected President. There were nearly sixty delegates present; and as they rose, in quick succession, to describe the state of their districts, it was evident they were, each and all, filled with the desire of keeping the people from returning to their labour. They believed the time had come for trying, successfully, to paralyse the Government . . . Thomas Cooper. *The Life of Thomas Cooper written by Himself*, 2nd edn, 190–1, 195, 206, 207–8. 1872

65 . . . I became an opponent to the reduction of wages to the bottom of my soul; and as long as I live I shall continue to keep up the wages of labour, to the utmost of my power . . .

. . . I will acknowledge and confess before you . . . that before I would have lived to submit to another reduction of 25 *per cent*, I would have terminated my own existence . . .

I was twenty years among the hand-loom weavers, and ten years in a factory, and I unhesitatingly say, that during the whole course of that time I worked twelve hours a day with the exception of twelve months that the masters of Stockport would not employ me; and the longer and harder I have worked the poorer and poorer I have become every year, until, at last, I am nearly exhausted. If the masters had taken off another 25 *per cent,* I would put an end to my existence sooner than kill myself working twelve hours a day in a cotton factory, and eating potatoes and salt . . . *The Lancaster Trials.* 1843

Changing Views on the Factory System   T. B. Macaulay, Whig politician, reviewer, Indian administrator and popular historian, was a bitter opponent of M. T. Sadler, both in the *Edinburgh Review* and on the 1832 Leeds hustings. By the mid-1840s, however, Macaulay had joined a Whiggish group which, while generally favouring an 11- rather than a 10-hours' measure, was committed to some further factory reform. His speech of 22 May 1846 on Fielden's Bill argued the question philosophically, balancing Britain's assured industrial greatness with her population's health and morality. He inevitably shocked the uncritical upholders of *laisser-faire.*

66   The details of the bill, Sir, will be more conveniently and more regularly discussed when we consider it in Committee. Our business at present is with the principle: and the principle, we are told by many gentlemen of great authority, is unsound. In their opinion, neither this bill, nor any other bill regulating the hours of labour, can be defended. This, they say, is one of those matters about which we ought not to legislate at all; one of those matters which settle themselves far better than any government can settle them. Now it is most important that this point should be fully cleared up. We certainly ought not to usurp functions which do not properly belong to us: but on the other hand, we ought not to abdicate functions which do properly belong to us. I hardly know which is the greater pest to society, a paternal government, that is to say a prying, meddlesome government, which intrudes itself into every part of human life, and which thinks that it can do everything for everybody better than anybody can do anything for himself; or a careless, lounging government, which suffers grievances, such as it could at once remove, to grow and multiply, and which to all complaint and remonstrance has only one answer: "We must let things alone: we must

let things take their course: we must let things find their level".
There is no more important problem in politics than to ascertain
the just mean between these two most pernicious extremes, to
draw correctly the line which divides those cases in which it is the
duty of the State to interfere from those cases in which it is the
duty of the State to abstain from interference. In old times the
besetting sin of rulers was undoubtedly an inordinate disposition
to meddle. The lawgiver was always telling people how to keep
their shops, how to till their fields, how to educate their children,
how many dishes to have on their tables, how much a yard to
give for the cloth which made their coats. He was always trying
to remedy some evil which did not properly fall within his
province; and the consequence was that he increased the evils
which he attempted to remedy. He was so much shocked by the
distress inseparable from scarcity that he made statutes against
forestalling and regrating, and so turned the scarcity into a
famine. He was so much shocked by the cunning and hard-
heartedness of moneylenders that he made laws against usury;
and the consequence was that the borrower, who, if he had been
left unprotected, would have got money at ten per cent, could
hardly, when protected, get it at fifteen per cent. Some eminent
political philosphers of the last century exposed with great
ability the folly, of such legislation, and, by doing so, rendered
a great service to mankind. There has been a reaction, a reaction
which has doubtless produced much good, but which, like most
reactions, has not been without evils and dangers. Our statesmen
cannot now be accused of being busybodies. But I am afraid
that there is, even in some of the ablest and most upright among
them, a tendency to the opposite fault . . .

. . . I am, I believe, as strongly attached as any member of this
House to the principle of free trade, rightly understood. Trade,
considered merely as trade, considered merely with reference to
the pecuniary interest of the contracting parties, can hardly be
too free. But there is a great deal of trade which cannot be considered merely as trade, and which affects higher than pecuniary
interests. And to say that Government never ought to regulate

such trade is a monstrous proposition, a proposition at which Adam Smith would have stood aghast . . .

And now, Sir, to come closer to the case with which we have to deal, I say, first, that where the health of the community is concerned, it may be the duty of the State to interfere with the contracts of individuals; and to this proposition I am quite sure that Her Majesty's Government will cordially assent . . .

Secondly, I say that where the public morality is concerned it may be the duty of the State to interfere with the contracts of individuals . . .

Will it be denied that the health of a large part of the rising generation may be seriously affected by the contracts which this bill is intended to regulate? Can any man who has read the evidence which is before us, can any man who has ever observed young people, can any man who remembers his own sensations when he was young, doubt that twelve hours a day of labour in a factory is too much for a lad of thirteen?

Or will it be denied that this is a question in which public morality is concerned? Can any one doubt,—none, I am sure, of my friends around me doubts,—that education is a matter of the highest importance to the virtue and happiness of a people? Now we know that there can be no education without leisure. It is evident that, after deducting from the day twelve hours for labour in a factory, and the additional hours necessary for exercise, refreshment, and repose, there will not remain time enough for education.

I have now, I think, shown that this bill is not in principle objectionable; and yet I have not touched the strongest part of our case. I hold that, where public health is concerned, and where public morality is concerned, the State may be justified in regulating even the contracts of adults. But we propose to regulate only the contracts of infants. Now was there ever a civilised society in which the contracts of infants were not under some regulation? Is there a single member of this House who will say that a wealthy minor of thirteen ought to be at perfect liberty to execute a conveyance of his estate, or to give a bond for fifty thousand pounds?... The minors whom we wish to protect have not indeed large property to throw away; but they are not the less our wards. Their only inheritance, the only fund to which they must look for their subsistence through life, is the sound mind in the sound body. And is it not our duty to prevent them from wasting that most precious wealth before they know its value?

But, it is said, this bill, though it directly limits only the labour of infants, will, by an indirect operation, limit also the labour of adults. Now, Sir, though I am not prepared to vote for a bill directly limiting the labour of adults, I will plainly say that I do not think that the limitation of the labour of adults would necessarily produce all those frightful consequences which we have heard predicted. You cheer me in very triumphant tones, as if I had uttered some monstrous paradox. Pray, does it not occur to any of you that the labour of adults is now limited in this country? Are you not aware that you are living in a society in which the labour of adults is limited to six days in seven? It is you, not I, who maintain a paradox opposed to the opinions and the practices of all nations and ages. Did you ever hear of a single civilised State since the beginning of the world in which a certain portion of time was not set apart for the rest and recreation of adults by public authority?...

Will my honourable friend the Member for Sheffield maintain that the law which limits the number of working days has been injurious to the working population? I am certain that he will not. How then can he expect me to believe that a law which limits the number of working hours must necessarily be injurious to the working population? Yet he and those who agree with him seem to wonder at our dullness because we do not at once admit the truth of the doctrine which they propound on this subject. They reason thus. We cannot reduce the number of hours of labour in factories without reducing the amount of production. We cannot reduce the amount of production without reducing the remuneration of the labourer. Meanwhile, foreigners, who are at liberty to work till they drop down dead at their looms, will soon beat us out of all the markets of the world. Wages will go down fast. The condition of our working people will be far worse than it is; and our unwise interference will, like the unwise interference of our ancestors with the dealings of the corn factor and the money lender, increase the distress of the very class which we wish to relieve.

Now, Sir, I fully admit that there might be such a limitation of the hours of labour as would produce the evil consequences with which we are threatened: and this, no doubt, is a very good reason for legislating with great caution, for feeling our way, for looking well to all the details of this bill. But it is certainly not true that every limitation of the hours of labour must produce these consequences. And I am, I must say, surprised when I hear men of eminent ability and knowledge lay down the proposition that a diminution of the time of labour must be followed by a diminution of the wages of labour, as a proposition capable of being strictly demonstrated, as a proposition about which there can be no more doubt than about any theorem in Euclid. Sir, I deny the truth of the proposition; and for this plain reason. We have already, by law, greatly reduced the time of labour in factories. Thirty years ago, the late Sir Robert Peel told the House that it was a common practice to make children of eight years of age toil in mills fifteen hours a day. A law has since been made which prohibits persons under eighteen years of age from working in mills more than twelve hours a day. That law was opposed on exactly the same grounds on which the bill before us is opposed. Parliament was told then, as it is told now, that with the time of labour the quantity of production would decrease, that with the quantity of production the wages would decrease, that our manufacturers would be unable to contend with foreign manufacturers, and that the condition of the labouring population instead of being made better by the interference of the Legislature would be made worse. Read over those debates; and you may imagine that you are reading the debate of this evening. Parliament disregarded these prophecies. The time of labour was limited. Have wages fallen? Has the cotton trade left Manchester for France or Germany? Has the condition of the working people become more miserable? Is it not universally acknowledged that the evils which were so confidently predicted have not come to pass? Let me be understood. I am not arguing that, because a law which reduced the hours of daily labour from fifteen to twelve did not reduce wages, a law reducing those hours from twelve to ten or eleven cannot possibly reduce wages. That would be very inconclusive reasoning. What I say is this, that, since a law which reduced the hours of daily labour from fifteen to twelve has not reduced wages, the proposition that every reduction of the hours of labour must necessarily reduce wages is a false proposition. There is evidently some flaw in that demonstration which my honourable friend thinks so complete . . .

. . . For my own part, I have not the smallest doubt that, if we and our ancestors had, during the last three centuries, worked just as hard on the Sundays as on the week days, we should have been at this moment a poorer people and a less civilised people than we are; that there would have been less production than there has been, that the wages of the labourer would have been lower than they are, and that some other nation would have been now making cotton stuffs and woollen stuffs and cutlery for the whole world.

Of course, Sir, I do not mean to say that a man will not produce more in a week by working seven days than by working six days. But I very much doubt whether, at the end of a year, he will generally have produced more by working seven days a week than by working six days a week; and I firmly believe that, at the end of twenty years, he will have produced much less by working seven days a week than by working six days a week. In the same manner I do not deny that a factory child will produce more, in a single day, by working twelve hours than by working ten hours, and by working fifteen hours than by working twelve hours. But I do deny that a great society in which children work fifteen, or even twelve hours a day, will in the lifetime of a generation, produce as much as if those children had worked less. If we consider man merely in a commercial point of view,

M

if we consider him merely as a machine for the production of worsted and calico, let us not forget what a piece of mechanism he is, how fearfully and wonderfully made. We do not treat a fine horse or a sagacious dog exactly as we treat a spinning jenny. Nor will any slaveholder, who has sense enough to know his own interest, treat his human chattels exactly as he treats his horses and his dogs. And would you treat the free labourer of England like a mere wheel or pulley? Rely on it that intense labour, beginning too early in life, continued too long every day, stunting the growth of the body, stunting the growth of the mind, leaving no time for healthful exercise, leaving no time for intellectual culture, must impair all those high qualities which have made our country great. Your overworked boys will become a feeble and ignoble race of men, the parents of a more feeble and more ignoble progeny; nor will it be long before the deterioration of the labourer will injuriously affect those very interests to which his physical and moral energies have been sacrificed. On the other hand, a day of rest recurring in every week, two or three hours of leisure, exercise, innocent amusement or useful study, recurring every day, must improve the whole man, physically, morally, intellectually; and the improvement of the man will improve all that the man produces. Why is it, Sir, that the Hindoo cotton manufacturer, close to whose door the cotton grows, cannot, in the bazaar of his own town, maintain a competition with the English cotton manufacturer, who has to send thousands of miles for the raw material, and who has then to send the wrought material thousands of miles to market? You will say that it is owing to the excellence of our machinery. And to what is the excellence of our machinery owing? How many of the improvements which have been made in our machinery do we owe to the ingenuity and patient thought of working men? Adam Smith tells us in the first chapter of his great work, that you can hardly go to a factory without seeing some very pretty machine, —that is his expression,—devised by some labouring man. Hargraves, the inventor of the spinning jenny, was a common artisan. Crompton, the inventor of the mule jenny, was a working man.

How many hours of the labour of children would do so much for our manufactures as one of these improvements has done? And in what sort of society are such improvements most likely to be made? Surely in a society in which the faculties of the working people are developed by education. How long will you wait before any negro, working under the lash in Louisiana, will contrive a better machinery for squeezing the sugar canes? My honorable friend seems to me, in all his reasonings about the commercial prosperity of nations, to overlook entirely the chief cause on which that prosperity depends. What is it, Sir, that makes the great difference between country and country? Not the exuberance of soil; not the mildness of climate; not mines, nor havens, nor rivers. These things are indeed valuable when put to their proper use by human intelligence: but human intelligence can do much without them; and they without human intelligence can do nothing. They exist in the highest degree in regions of which the inhabitants are few, and squalid, and barbarous, and naked, and starving; while on sterile rocks, amidst unwholesome marshes, and under inclement skies, may be found immense populations, well fed, well lodged, well clad, well governed. Nature meant Egypt and Sicily to be the gardens of the world. They once were so. Is it anything in the earth or in the air that makes Scotland more prosperous than Egypt, that makes Holland more prosperous than Sicily? No; it was the Scotchman that made Scotland: it was the Dutchman that made Holland ... Man, man is the great instrument that produces wealth. The natural difference between Campania and Spitzbergen is trifling when compared with the difference between a country inhabited by men full of bodily and mental vigour, and a country inhabited by men sunk in bodily and mental decrepitude. Therefore it is that we are not poorer but richer, because we have, through many ages, rested from our labour one day in seven. That day is not lost. While industry is suspended, while the plough lies in the furrow, while the Exchange is silent, while no smoke ascends from the factory, a process is going on quite as important to the wealth of nations as any process which is performed on more

busy days. Man, the machine of machines, the machine compared with which all the contrivances of the Watts and the
Arkwrights are worthless, is repairing and winding up, so that he
returns to his labours on the Monday with clearer intellect, with
livelier spirits, with renewed corporal vigour. Never will I believe that what makes a population stronger, and healthier, and
wiser, and better, can ultimately make it poorer. You try to
frighten us by telling us that, in some German factories, the
young work seventeen hours in the twenty-four, that they work
so hard that among thousands there is not one who grows to such
a stature that he can be admitted into the army; and you ask
whether, if we pass this bill, we can possibly hold our own against
such competition as this? Sir, I laugh at the thought of such
competition. If ever we are forced to yield the foremost place
among commercial nations, we shall yield it, not to a race of
degenerate dwarfs, but to some people preeminently vigorous in
body and in mind. *Speeches of the Right Honorable T. B. Macaulay,
M.P., corrected by himself,* 436–7, 439, 440, 442–4, 447–9, 450–4.
1854

The *Manchester Guardian*, founded as a weekly liberal journal in
1821, became a prominent mouthpiece of the Northern manufacturers though it was periodically challenged by more radical
rivals. It strongly opposed factory legislation in the 1830s,
gradually altering its views as legislation was passed. The
following extracts show some of the *Guardian's* later changes of
attitude.

67   The Ten Hours Factories Bill.

As the measure receives the modified support of the most influential members of the government, it appears probable that
it will be read a second time, but that in committee it will, in
accordance with their opinion, be converted into an eleven
hours' bill, and in this form receive the sanction of the legislature.

Our opinions on this subject are well known to our readers. No
exertions are made by the workpeople to effect, by arrangements

with their masters, any diminution in the hours of labour, an object which they might easily accomplish, if they really desired it; and we thence infer that they are not prepared to submit to any reduction of their earnings, but that they support the Ten Hours Bill in the belief that under its operation their wages would remain undiminished. This opinion we believe to be most unfounded . . .

. . . But while we concur with Mr. Bright in opposing the Ten Hours Bill, we cannot join with him in thinking that its enactment would involve any violation of principle . . .

On the other hand, it appears to us that Lord John Russell, in replying to Mr. Bright, treated the apprehensions of foreign competition much too lightly . . . we believe that the diminution it [the Bill] would cause in the powers of production would be most injurious to the manufacturing supremacy of England.

17 February 1847

The Ten Hours' Bill

. . . The probability is, that the bill will be carried as it now stands . . . There certainly never was a time, in the history of the cotton manufacture, when a limitation to ten hours would interfere less with the engagements of the masters, or the earnings of the workpeople, than the period now before us . . .

20 February 1847

The Factory Act

We should be very glad to see the long hours of labour which have prevailed in a few mills in different parts of the country . . . effectually put down, either by legislation or public opinion; and one great objection which we have always felt to the Ten Hours Act was, the temptation which it held out to an evasion of its provisions . . .

27 April 1850

The ever-active Robert Baker not only helped to administer the Factory Acts but also sought to explain and justify them. In the following extracts he looks back, in the 1850s, at the achievements of factory legislation.

68 TO THE FACTORY OCCUPIERS AND FACTORY WORKERS OF THE UNITED KINGDOM.

The Factory Laws have been passed with a view to educate the young, and to fix such a reasonable limit to the hours of labour, that the workers under them may not only be protected physically, but have time for mental and social improvement also.

By these laws, restrictions have been placed upon the capital of the masters, and responsibilities on their servants and upon the parents of children, both of which were necessary for the well-being of the manufacturing districts. Excessive labour had at one time produced a class of diseases peculiar to the factory system, which have greatly *decreased under its present limitation*; whilst thousands of children have been, and are now being educated under the Factory Acts, who otherwise would never have been educated at all. But there is a great deal more yet to be done. There is not only to maintain that physical protection, and thereby to increase the duration of life amongst the factory workers, which is very nearly the lowest amongst the English work-people,—but there is also an immense moral regeneration to be accomplished, antagonistic of the effects of a mixed congregation, for which, time, and the co-operation of Inspectors, Masters, and Workpeople, are alike and absolutely necessary. My experience, as Medical Inspector of many large factories prior to the passing of the Factory Acts, and my official connection with them since, enable me to speak positively on these points; and to wish also that these useful powers could be extended to many other branches of infant labour. Robert Baker. *The Factory Acts Made Easy: or, How To Work the Law Without Risk of Penalties*, iii–iv. Leeds 1854

69 ... There were in 1856, and there are at the present moment, employed within the factories of the United Kingdom, 682,517 persons, compared with 354,684 in 1835. Of these 387,826 are females, compared with 167,696 in 1835; and 46,071 are children between eight and thirteen years of age, as compared with 56,455. There is thus a gross increase of workers of 92 per cent.: the increase of females being 131 per cent., and nearly as many children as there were formerly; and yet all the diseases which were specific to factory labour in 1832 have as nearly as possible disappeared. We seldom or never now see a case of in-knee or of flat-foot; occasionally one of slight curvature of the spine, arising more from labour with poor food than from labour specifically. The factory leg is no more amongst us, except as an old man or woman who limps by, to remind one of the fearful past, or of the more rational and social present. The faces of the people are ruddy, their forms are rounded, their very appearance is a joyous one; and although it is not attempted to be denied that, even with the present hours of work, in weakly and scrofulous constitutions, factory labour like any other kind of labour, may induce occasional deformity, yet so much carefulness is exercised by the certifying surgeons in passing only healthy children, that they are extremely rare, and the sufferers are never permitted to continue at work.

... It is extremely gratifying to find that an experiment which had many opponents when it was about to be tried, has been productive of such great benefit to the working classes, without, I believe, an atom of either personal, commercial, or national wrong.

... And whilst England, whose wealth is in her commerce, may rejoice that she had the courage to seemingly put fetters on that commerce, when the physical health of her people was endangered, she may rejoice also that in doing so she brought to life that other principle of national greatness, without which the former would be comparatively nothing worth—viz., the means of extending the intellectual and of promoting the social happiness of so many of her sons and daughters; and they, too, who, amidst many trials, difficulties, and prejudices, promoted that law at great expense and with many personal sacrifices, and carried it to a successful issue, may rejoice in the good which it has effected. Their names are everywhere cherished with the most grateful recollections, and their memories will be imperishable. Robert Baker. 'On the Physical Effects of Diminished Labour', *Transactions of the National Association for the Promotion of Social Science*, 558, 561, 563. 1859

Although given to exaggerating his own rôle and by implication minimising the importance of the factory agitation in the textile districts, Ashley (from 1851 the 7th Earl of Shaftesbury) could look back on a long career of humanitarian service. Late in life, he recalled the difficulties which had faced him. In the following extract from his memorandum Shaftesbury seriously underrates the strength of Church support in the North, but fairly recalls some of his opponents' actions.

70 . . . I had to break every political connection, to encounter a most formidable array of capitalists, mill-owners, doctrinaires, and men, who, by natural impulse, hate all "humanity-mongers". They easily influence the ignorant, the timid, and the indifferent; and my strength lay at first ("tell it not in Gath!") among the Radicals, the Irishmen, and a few sincere Whigs and Conservatives. Peel was hostile, though, in his cunning, he concealed the full extent of his hostility until he took the reins of office, and then he opposed me, not with decision only but malevolence, threatening, he and Graham, to break up his administration and "retire into private life" unless the House of Commons rescinded the vote it had given in favour of my Ten Hours Bill. The Tory country gentlemen reversed their votes; but, in 1847, indignant with Peel on the ground of Corn Law repeal, they returned to the cause of the factory children.

Fielden and Brotherton were the only "practical" men, as the phrase then went, who supported me, and to the "practical" prophecies of overthrow of trade, of ruin to the operatives themselves, I could only oppose "humanity" and general principles. The newspapers were, on the whole, friendly; some very much so. A few, especially the local journals, inconceivably bitter, though balanced by local papers sound and hearty in their support.

Out of Parliament, there was in society, every form of "good-natured" and compassionate contempt. In the provinces, the anger and irritation of the opponents were almost fearful; and men among first classes of workpeople, overlookers and others, were afraid to avow their sentiments. It required, during many years, repeated journeys to Lancashire and Yorkshire, no end of public meetings in the large towns; visits, committees, innumerable hours, intolerable expense. In very few instances did any mill-owner appear on the platform with me; in still fewer the ministers of any religious denomination. At first not one, except the Rev. Mr. Bull, of Bierley, near Bradford; and even to the last, very few, so cowed were they (or in themselves so indifferent) by the overwhelming influence of the cotton lords.

I had much more aid from the medical than the divine profession; and ever must I record the services and skill of Mr. Fletcher of Bury.

The demands upon time and strength were quite up to my powers, and, indeed, much beyond them. I suffered a good deal.

The operatives themselves did their duty. Their delegates, whom they maintained at their own cost, were always active and trustworthy men: specially my friend and fellow-labourer, Philip Grant, who was, in my support, as two right hands.

Perhaps the various efforts made by Sir R. Peel to induce me to take office were amongst the greatest of my difficulties . . .

. . . I started to assail home interests, with every one, save a few unimposing persons, against me. O'Connell was a sneering and bitter opponent; Gladstone ever voted in resistance to my efforts; and Brougham played the doctrinaire in the House of Lords.

Bright was ever my most malignant opponent. Cobden, though bitterly hostile, was better than Bright. He abstained from opposition on the Collieries Bill, and gave positive support on the Calico Print-works Bill.

Gladstone is on a level with the rest; he gave no support to the

Ten Hours Bill; he voted with Sir R. Peel to rescind the famous decision in favour of it. He was the only member who endeavoured to delay the Bill which delivered women and children from mines and pits; and never did he say a word on behalf of the factory children, until, *when defending slavery in the West Indies*, he taunted Buxton with indifference to the slavery in England!

Lord Brougham was among my most heated opponents. He spoke strongly against the Bill in 1847.

Miss Martineau also gave her voice and strength in resistance to the measure.

By degrees some public men came round. Russell, then Lord John, did me disservice while he was Minister; he espoused the cause when turned into Opposition. Then Sir G. Grey adhered; and, towards the end, Macaulay gave us one of his brilliant and effective speeches. My latter years in the House of Commons were dogged by Oastler and the Fieldens, who resented my policy in bringing all things to a happy conclusion by making and accepting concessions to abate too much exultation in the operatives, and too much soreness in the mill-owners.

The pressure upon purse and upon time was very great; the pressure upon strength was greater, but the pressure on the mind was greatest of all. I endured terrible anxieties.

(I have omitted from the above that the famous O'Connell was, for a long time, very bitter and hostile, and spoke of the "good-natured nonsense" I delivered. He became, afterwards, much milder.) Sir Edwin Hodder. *The Life and Work of the Seventh Earl of Shaftesbury, K.G.*, 3 vols, II, 209–10. 1886

Industry's Triumph   The Great Exhibition was officially opened in the Crystal Palace in Hyde Park on 1 May 1851. Goods of all sorts—roughly half British and Imperial and half foreign—were shown by over 13,000 exhibitors to over 6,000,000 visitors during its five months of life. Hated by the arch-enemy of industry, Colonel Waldo Sibthorp, MP for Lincoln, and energetically patronised by the Prince Consort, the Exhibition was an enormous success. It stressed both the Free Traders' belief in peace through competition and the great development of British Industry. The confident years as the world's workshop lay ahead. Journalistic descriptions of the opening ceremony mirrored the national wonder.

---

71 There was yesterday witnessed a sight the like of which has never happened before, and which, in the nature of things, can never be repeated. They who were so fortunate as to see it hardly knew what most to admire, or in what form to clothe the sense of wonder, and even of mystery, which struggled within them. The edifice, the treasures of nature and art collected therein, the assemblage, and the solemnity of the occasion, all conspired to suggest something even more than sense could scan or imagination attain. There were many there who were familiar with magnificent spectacles; who had seen coronations, fetes, and solemnities; but they had not seen anything to compare with this. In a building that could easily have accommodated twice as many, twenty-five thousand persons, so it is computed, were arranged in order round the throne of our SOVEREIGN. Around them, amidst them, and over their heads was displayed all that is useful or beautiful in nature or in art. Above them rose a glittering arch far more lofty and spacious than the vaults of even our noblest cathedrals. On either side the vista seemed almost boundless . . .

. . . We do not see why every child whom its parents can bring up to town should not take lessons at the Exhibition. But in this branch of knowledge it is not uncommon to find grown up people as ill informed as their own children. All ages therefore will find it to their advantage to go to school for the season in Hyde Park. *The Times*, 2 May 1851

Notes

PART ONE: THE CONSEQUENCES OF THE FACTORY SYSTEM

Artisans and Machinery On other working-class reactions to machinery see parts 2 and 3 *infra*. Gaskell's book has been reprinted, 1968; his original work was *The Manufacturing Population of England*, 1833. For the statistics justifying liberal writers' general optimism see G. R. Porter. *The Progress of the Nation* (1847 edn); and B. R. Mitchell and Phyllis Deane. *Abstract of British Historical Statistics*. Cambridge, 1962. On Babbage see M. Moseley. *Irascible Genius.* 1964.

Industrial Health On Thackrah see A. Meiklejohn. *The Life, Work and Times of C. T. Thackrah.* Edinburgh, 1957; on Kay, Frank Smith. *The Life of Sir James Kay-Shuttleworth*, 1923; on Baker, Frank Beckwith, 'Robert Baker', *University of Leeds Review*, vii, 1960; W. R. Lee, 'Robert Baker: The First Doctor in the Factory Department', *British Journal of Industrial Medicine*, xxi, 1964.

The Factory Town On Jones see John Saville. *Ernest Jones, Chartist*, 1952. Bradford awaits its modern historian, but William Cudworth. *Round about Bradford*. Bradford, 1876; *Rambles round Horton*. Bradford, 1886; *Histories of Bolton and Bowling*. Bradford, 1891; *Manningham, Heaton and Allerton*. Bradford, 1896; may be consulted. On Manchester see Léon Faucher, *Manchester in 1844: Its Present Condition and Future Prospects*, 1844, 1968; Archibald Prentice. *Historical Sketches and Personal Recollections of Manchester*, 1851; intro Donald Read, 1970; T. S. Ashton. *Economic and Social Investigations in Manchester, 1833–1933*, 1934; W. H.

Chaloner. 'The Birth of Modern Manchester', in British Association handbook *Manchester and Its Region*, 1962; Asa Briggs. *Victorian Cities*, 1963, 1968; Donald Read. *The English Provinces*, 1964. On the great Manchester firm founded in 1797 by James McConnell and John Kennedy see J. McConnell. *A Century of Fine Spinning*. Manchester, 1906. Disraeli's novels have regularly been reprinted. See also W. F. Monypenny, *The Life of Benjamin Disraeli*, ii (1912) ch 7, 9; M. E. Speare. *The Political Novel*. New York, 1924; M. Masefield. *Peacocks and Primroses*, 1953; Robert Blake. *Disraeli*, 1966, 'Disraeli's Political Novels', *History Today*, xvi, 1966.

Factory Life For varied contemporary views see J. T. Ward. *The Factory Movement, 1830–1855*, 1962. On Blinco see A. E. Musson. 'Robert Blinco and the Early Factory System', *Derbyshire Miscellany*, 1957. Dodd's *Narrative* has been republished with his *Factory System Illustrated*, 1842; intro W. H. Chaloner, 1968. On Sadler see *Memoirs of the Life and Writings of M. T. Sadler*, 1842; J. T. Ward, 'M. T. Sadler', *University of Leeds Review*, vii, 1960. Myles' book has been reissued twice, Dundee, 1887, 1951. On Myles see W. Norrie. *Dundee Celebrities of the Nineteenth Century*, 132–3. Dundee, 1873.

Visits to the Factories On Roebuck see R. E. Leader. *The Life and Letters of J. A. Roebuck*, 1897; on Mrs Trollope, T. A. Trollope. *What I Remember*, 1887, E. Bigland. *The Indomitable Mrs Trollope*, 1953, W. H. Chaloner. 'Mrs Trollope and the Early Factory System', *Victorian Studies*, iv, 1960. A selection from Simond's book has been published (ed Christopher Hibbert) as *An American in Regency England*, 1968; Mrs Trollope's novel has been reissued, 1968; Cooke Taylor's book has been republished (intro W. H. Chaloner, 1968). For a selection of foreign comments see W. O. Henderson. *Industrial Britain under the Regency*, 1968.

PART TWO: FACTORY REFORM
Child Labour See O. J. Dunlop, R. D. Denman, *English Apprenticeship and Child Labour*, 1912; B. L. Hutchins, A. Harrison. *History of Factory Legislation*, 1926, 1967; on female labour,

W. F. Neff. *Victorian Working Women*, 1929, and Ivy Pinchbeck. *Women Workers and the Industrial Revolution, 1750–1850*, 1930. Wesley's views are given in his *Journal*; see also W. J. Warner. *Wesleyan Movement in the Industrial Revolution*, 1930; E. R.Taylor. *Methodism and Politics*. Cambridge, 1935; R. F. Wearmouth. *Some Working Class Movements* . . . 1948; R. G. Cowherd. *The Politics of English Dissent*, 1959. On Crompton see M. E. Rose. 'Samuel Crompton . . . A Reconsideration', *Transactions of the Lancashire and Cheshire Antiquarian Soc*, lxxv–lxxvi, 1969.

The Leadership of Richard Oastler The best biography of Oastler is Cecil Driver. *Tory Radical. The Life of Richard Oastler*. New York, 1946; on the 'Fixby Compact' see W. R. Croft. *The History of the Factory Movement*. Huddersfield, 1888; D. F. E. Sykes. *History of Huddersfield*. Huddersfield, 1898; J. T. Ward, 'Some Industrial Reformers', *Bradford Textile Soc Jour*, 1962–3.

The Factory Reformers On regional agitations and agitators see J. T. Ward. 'Matthew Balme (1813–1884) Factory Reformer', *Bradford Antiquary* ns xl, 1960; 'Squire Auty (1812–1870)', ibid, xliii, 1964; 'Bradford and Factory Reform', *Bradford Textile Soc Jour*, 1960–1; 'Leeds and the Factory Reform Movement', *Publications of the Thoresby Society*, xlvi, 1961; 'The Factory Reform Movement in Scotland', *Scott Hist Rev*, xli, 1962; 'The Factory Movement in Lancashire, 1830–1850', *Transactions of the Lancashire and Cheshire Antiquarian Society*, lxxv–lxxvi, 1969. On the Church's attitude see W. R. W. Stephens. *Life and Letters of W. F. Hook*, 1879; C. J. Stranks. *Dean Hook*, 1954; J. C. Gill. *The Ten Hours Parson*, 1959, and *Parson Bull of Byerley*, 1963.

The Ten Hours Bill On Hobhouse (later 1st Lord Broughton) see Lord Broughton (ed Lady Dorchester). *Recollections of a Long Life*, 1909–11; Michael Joyce, *My Friend H*, 1948. On the first Leeds election see A. S. Turberville, Frank Beckwith. 'Leeds and Parliamentary Reform, 1820–1832', *Pub Thoresby Soc*, xli, 1943; Asa Briggs, 'The Background of the Parliamentary Reform Movement in Three English Cities', *Cambridge Historical Journal*, x, 1952. Kydd's book has been republished, 1967, along with the Commissioners' First Report, 1968.

The Factory Reform Agitation On the operation of the 1833 Act see D. H. Blelloch. 'A Historical Survey of Factory Inspection in Great Britain', *International Labour Review*, 1938; T. K. Djang. *Factory Inspection in Great Britain*, 1942, 1968; M. W. Thomas. *The Early Factory Legislation*, Leigh-on-Sea, 1948. On Stephens see G. J. Holyoake. *Life of J. R. Stephens*, 1881; J. T. Ward, 'Revolutionary Tory: The Life of Joseph Rayner Stephens of Ashton-under-Lyne (1805–1879)', *Trans Lancs & Chesh Antiq Soc*, lxviii, 1958.

The Propaganda Battle On Fielden see Francis Espinasse in *Dictionary of National Biography*, xviii, 1889; Joshua Holden. *A Short History of Todmorden*. Manchester, 1912; G. D. H. Cole. *Chartist Portraits*, 1941, intro Asa Briggs 1965. On Horner, see K. M. Lyell. *Memoir of Leonard Horner*, 1890. Fielden's book has been republished (intro J. T. Ward, 1969) and Wing's book has been reissued, 1967. Major collections of reformers' publications are Oastler's 'White Slavery' collection (16 vols in the Goldsmiths' Library, London University, 6 vols in Columbia University Library, New York) and Matthew Balme's collection (Bradford City Reference Library).

The Later Movement The best biography of Ashley is still Sir Edwin Hodder. *Life and Work of the Seventh Earl of Shaftesbury*, 1886, 1887. Less reliable accounts are given in J. W. Bready. *Lord Shaftesbury and Social-Economic Progress*, 1923, and J. L. and B. Hammond. *Lord Shaftesbury*, 1923, 1968; see also Norman Gash. 'Ashley and the Conservative Party in 1842', *Eng Hist Rev*, liii, 1938; and, on Graham, J. T. Ward. *Sir James Graham*, 1967.

PART THREE: THE FACTORY SYSTEM AND
SOCIETY

The Masters' Case See W. H. Hutt. 'The Factory System of the Early Nineteenth Century', *Economica*, vi, 1929, reprinted in F. A. Hayek (ed) *Capitalism and the Historians*, 1954; Sir J. H. Clapham. *An Economic History of Modern Britain*, Cambridge, 1926–38. The literature on the associated controversy over workers' living standards is vast. For a selection of recent comments see T. S. Ashton. 'Some Statistics of the Industrial Revolution in Britain', *The Manchester School*, xvi, 1948, 'The Standard of Life of the Workers in England, 1790–1830', *Jour Econ Hist*, Supp ix, 1949; A. J. Taylor. 'Progress and Poverty in Britain, 1780–1850: A Reappraisal', *History*, xlv, 1960; R. M. Hartwell, 'The Rising Standard of Living in England, 1800–1850', *Econ Hist Rev*, 2s, xiv, 1961; R. M. Hartwell and E. J. Hobsbawm, 'The Standard of Living during the Industrial Revolution', ibid, xvi, 1963; E. J. Hobsbawm, 'The British Standard of Living 1790–1850', ibid, x, 1957, *Labouring Men*, 1964, *Industry and Empire*, 1968; J. E. Williams. 'The British Standard of Living, 1750–1850', *Econ Hist Rev* 2s, xix, 1966.

The 'Intellectual' Attitude On Senior see Marion Bowley. *Nassau Senior and Classical Economics*, 1937; on Place, Graham Wallas. *The Life of Francis Place*, 1918. The error in Senior's calculations is pointed out in Knut Wicksell (ed Lord Robbins). *Lectures on Political Economy*, i, 194–5, 1935. See also E. R. A. Seligman. 'On Some Neglected British Economists', *Econ Jour*, xiii, 1903; K. O. Walker. 'The Classical Economists and the Factory Acts', *Jour Econ Hist*, i, 1941; J. B. Brebner. 'Laisser Faire and State Intervention in 19th Century Britain', ibid, Supp viii, 1948; L. R. Sorenson. 'Some Classical Economists, Laisser Faire and the Factory Acts', ibid, xii, 1952; S. A. Meenai. 'Robert Torrens, 1780–1864', *Economica*, xxiii, 1956; Mark Blaug, 'The Classical Economists and the Factory Acts: A Re-Examination', *Quarterly Journal of Economics*, lxxiii, 1958; S. C. Deb. 'British Factory Movement in the Early Nineteenth Century—Its Social and Economic Background', *Indian Journal of Economics*, xliv, 1963.

The Operation of Factory Legislation See notes to part 2 'The Factory Reform Agitation', *supra*; Reports of Factory Inspectors; J. M. Ludlow, L. Jones. *Progress of the Working Class, 1832–1867*, 1867; cf John Wade. *History of the Middle and Working Classes*, 1833, 1968; on factory education see A. H. Robson. *The Education of Children engaged in Industry, 1833–1876*, 1931; Gertrude Ward. 'Education of Factory Child Workers, 1833–50',

Econ Hist, iii, 1935; W. C. R. Hicks, 'Education of the Half-
Timer', ibid, iv, 1939; J. T. Ward, 'A Lost Opportunity in
Education: 1843', *Researches and Studies*, 20, 1959; W. H. G.
Armytage. *Four Hundred Years of English Education*, Cambridge,
1964; J. T. Ward and J. H. Treble. 'Religion and Education in
1843: Reaction to the Factory Education Bill', *Journal of
Ecclesiastical History*, xx, 1969.
Working-Class Organisations On oaths see E. P. Thomp-
son. *The Making of the English Working Class*, 1963. On Luddism
see also J. L. and B. Hammond. *The Skilled Labourer*, 1919; F. O.
Darvall. *Popular Disturbances and Public Order in Regency England*,
Oxford, 1934. On the unions see S. and B. Webb. *The History
of Trade Unionism*, 1950 impr; G. D. H. Cole. *Attempts at General
Union, 1818-1834*, 1953; Henry Pelling. *A History of British Trade
Unionism*, 1963. On Doherty, see Cole. *Chartist Portraits*. On the
'plug plot' see G. S. R. Kitson Clarke. 'Hunger and Politics in
1842', *Journal of Modern History*, xxv, 1953; A. G. Rose, 'The
Plug Plots of 1842 in Lancashire and Cheshire', *Trans Lancs &
Chesh Antiq Soc*, lxvii, 1957; F. C. Mather, *Public Order in the Age
of the Chartists*, Manchester, 1959; Ward, *Factory Movement*.
Peel's book has been republished (intro E. P. Thompson, 1968).
Changing Views on the Factory System On Macaulay
see G. O. Trevelyan. *Life and Letters of Lord Macaulay*, 1900 edn;
on the *Manchester Guardian*, Donald Read. *Press and People*, 1961;
on Baker notes to part 1 'Industrial Health', *supra*. For other
views on the effects of legislation see Ward. *Factory Movement*.
Industry's Triumph Much literature was issued on the
occasion of the 1851 Exhibition and for its centenary. The
setting is succinctly described in Asa Briggs. *1851*. Historical
Association, 1951. Professor Briggs' *Age of Improvement* is the best
general textbook for the whole period. On reactions see E. M.
Sigsworth. 'The West Riding Wool Textile Industry and the
Great Exhibition', *Yorkshire Bulletin of Economic and Social
Research*, iv, 1952; Christopher Sykes. 'Colonel Sibthorp: A
Festival Centenary', *History Today*, i, 1951; Audrey Short.
'Workers under Glass in 1851', *Victorian Studies*, x, 1966.

N

Index

Acts of Parliament: Calico Print-works (1845), 185; Collieries (1842), 185–6; Combination (1799, 1800), 157, 167; Combination repeal (1824), 157; Factory (1819), 27, 66; (1825), 66–7; (1829), 67; (1831), 91–3, 95, 98, 108, 122, 149; (1833), 19, 52, 54–5, 87, 106, 113, 116–20, 122, 124–31, 143, 145–8, 151–2, 161–2, 164–5, 176–7, 182–4; (1844), 84, 133–4, 137–9, 165–7; (1847), 54–6, 136–9, 162–4, 180–1; (1850), 136, 186; Health and Morals of Apprentices (1802), 66; New Poor Law (1834), 118, 120, 132, 146, 160; Public Health (1848), 29–30; Reform (1832), 96, 99, 103, 157; Registration (1836), 161; Truck (1831), 46; *see also* Corn Laws, Poor Laws
Albert, Prince Consort, 11, 186
Althorp, Viscount (3rd Earl Spencer), 11, 186
Anti-Corn Law League, 60, 62, 140, 170
Arbroath, 91
Arkwright, Sir Richard, 13, 180
Arnold, Thomas, 14
Ashley, Viscount (7th Earl of Shaftesbury), 59, 84, 85, 87, 102, 104, 120–2, 124, 126, 132–6, 144, 147, 159, 160, 165, 169, 184–6
Ashton, Thomas, 63, 83
Ashton-under-Lyne, 83–5, 118, 169

Ashworth, Edmund, 61–2, 146, 149
Ashworth, Henry, 61–3, 146
Astley, 83

Babbage, Charles, 14, 24–6, 146
Baines, Edward, 91, 95–6, 112, 113
Baines, (Sir) Edward, 113, 158–61
Balme, Matthew, 134
Baker, Robert, 30, 161–5, 181–4
Baxter, family, 48
Bentham, Jeremy, 104
Bethel, Richard, 75
Bierley, 60, 88, 91, 185
Bingley, 42, 82
Birley, Joseph, 140–1
Birmingham, 88
Blackburn, 116, 146
Blinco, Robert, 44
Bolton, 62, 146, 164
Bowring, Sir John, 12
Bradford, 31, 33–7, 73–6, 88, 91, 95, 112–13, 115–16, 130, 161, 185
Bright, John, 62, 140, 181, 185
British Association, 38
Brotherton, Joseph, 83–4, 184
Brougham, Henry (1st Lord), 74–5, 185–6
Broughton, 40
Brown, John, 44
Buckley, John, 34
Bull, George Stringer, 60, 88–91, 102, 114, 185
Byron, 6th Lord, 98
Bury, 185

Cambridge University, 24, 146

Campbell, John, 170–1

Carlyle, Thomas, 37

Chadwick, Sir Edwin, 29, 104

Charlestown, 120

Chartists, 32, 48, 80, 91, 118, 132, 140, 169–71

Cheetham, 40

Cheshire, 68, 125, 143, 167

Child labour, 15, 18–20, 27–9, 32–3, 44, 50–8, 60–1, 63, 66, 68–82, 88–9, 95–9, 104–8, 110–13, 115–17, 122–5, 128–31, 137–42, 155–6, 161–5, 174–9

Cholera, 29

Chorlton, 40

Church of England, 13, 67, 73, 80–2, 87–91, 98, 114, 129, 133, 158, 184–5; *see also* Evangelicals, Tractarians

Church of Scotland, 48

(Episcopal) Church of Scotland, 48

Cobbett, John, 136

Cobbett, William, 120

Cobden, Richard, 12, 185

Condy, George, 142

Congleton, 68

Congregationalists, 37, 158

Cooper, Thomas, 170–1

Corn Laws, 13, 101–2, 111, 135, 140, 170, 184

Cotton industry, 12, 17, 28–9, 34–7, 44, 56–68, 70, 76, 83–7, 91, 98, 120, 140–1, 146–52, 155, 157–8, 168–9, 176, 181, 185

Coulson, Samuel, 71–2

Crabtree, Geoffrey, 103–4

Crimean War, 13

Croker, John Wilson, 170

Crompton, George, 67–8

Crompton, Samuel, 62, 67, 178

Croppers, 167

Cumberland, 125

Cunliffe-Lister, Ellis, 13

Darwin, Erasmus, 14

Dawsholm printfield, 46–8

Derbyshire, 44, 125

Disraeli, Benjamin (1st Earl of Beaconsfield), 14, 41–4

Dodd, William, 44

Doherty, John, 85–7, 168–9

Dublin, 37, 40

Dukinfield, 83, 85

Dunckley, Henry, 13, 14,

Duncombe, William (2nd Lord Feversham), 75, 135

Dundee, 48, 50–6, 115

Durham, 125

Earnings, 51, 54–7, 64–6, 72, 144, 148, 152, 155, 161, 169, 171, 176–7, 181

Eccleshill, 36

Edinburgh University, 125

Edwards, Sir Henry, 1st Bt, 13

Egerton mill, 64

Eglinton, 14th Earl of, 13

Elliott, Ebenezer, 14

Emscot, 70

Escher, Hans, 12

Evangelicals, 66, 80

Factory Commission (1833), 18, 88–91, 103–8, 122, 124–5

Factory Inspectors, 68–9, 106, 122, 124–7, 136, 139, 144–5, 161–7, 181–4

Factory Reformation Society, 113

Factory Superintendents, 125, 145, 161, 165

Faucher, Leon, 17

Ferrand, William Busfeild, 42, 82, 135–6

Fielden, John, 13, 120–4, 135, 144, 172, 184

Fielden, John, jr, 120, 136, 186

Fielden, Joshua, 120, 136, 186

Fielden, Samuel, 120, 136, 186

Finishers, 22

Fixby, 73, 76, 79, 94

Flax, 12, 28, 46, 48, 93, 98–9, 104, 125, 141

Fletcher, Matthew, 185
Forbes, Thomas, 83
French, Gilbert J., 67–8
Friendly Societies, 26, 167

Gardner, Robert, 146
Gaskell, Peter, 18–22
George III, King, 91
Gisborne, Thomas, 103
Gladstone, William Ewart, 185–6
Glamis, 48–9
Glasgow, 46–8, 56–8, 146, 168
Goodman, Sir George, 116–18
Gould, Nathaniel, 66
Graham, Sir James (2nd Bt), 132–4,
 158, 160, 170, 184
Grant, Philip, 85, 87, 185
Great Exhibition, 11, 140, 186–7
Green, Henry, 134
Greg, Robert Hyde, 143–6
Greg, Samuel, 143
Greg, William Rathbone, 117, 143
Grey, Sir George, (2nd Bt), 136, 186
Guest, Richard, 22–4

Halifax, 95
Hamilton, Richard Winter, 73
Handloom weavers, 12, 24, 42, 51,
 110–11, 155, 171
Hardy, John, 35
Hargreaves, James, 178
Harwood, Philip, 11–13
Health, 26–31, 40, 55, 69, 77, 83, 90,
 99–100, 105–7, 122–4, 151–2, 174,
 178, 183
Health of Towns Association, 29
Heywood, 136
Hindley, Charles, 83–7
Hobhouse, Sir John Cam, 2nd Bt
 (1st Lord Broughton), 66, 73, 76–
 7, 91–8, 122, 142, 149
Hobson, Joshua, 116
Horner, Leonard, 125–9, 136, 145–
 7, 152, 161, 164
Horton, 36
Houldsworth, Thomas, 42
Howell, Thomas Jones, 161, 166

Huddersfield, 73, 76, 78–9, 92, 95,
 135
Hume, Joseph, 157
Hyde, 63, 118

Inglis, Sir Robert Harry, 2nd Bt,
 160
Ireland, 40, 48, 56, 109, 113, 125,
 184

James, John, 33–7
Jenkins, David, 129
Jones, David, 164
Jones, Ernest, 32–3
Jones, John, 41–2
Jute industry, 12, 48

Kay-Shuttleworth, Sir James Phil-
 lips, 1st Bt, 26–7
Keighley, 71, 130, 133–4
Kenyon, 2nd Lord, 66
Kennedy, John, 41–2, 189
Kenworthy, William, 146
Knaresborough, 82
Kydd, Samuel, 91–8

Lancashire, 39, 59, 62, 64, 83, 85,
 113, 120, 125–6, 134, 136, 146,
 157, 164, 167, 170, 185
Lee, George Augustus, 42
Leeds, 27, 30, 32, 70, 73, 91, 92, 95,
 98–9, 104–5, 109, 114, 116, 159–
 60, 162–4, 172
Leicester, 170
Liberals, 61–2, 73, 77–9, 109, 112,
 114, 116–17, 143, 146, 158, 180
Linen industry: see Flax
Liverpool, 39
London, 11, 146, 157
London University, 125
Luddism, 21, 167–8

Malthus, Thomas Robert, 99, 146
Manchester, 12, 14, 17, 26–7, 29,
 37–41, 66, 85–7, 105, 108, 113–14,
 120, 124, 140–1, 143, 151–2, 156,
 164, 168–71, 176, 180–1

Macaulay, Thomas Babington (1st
    Lord), 99, 113, 172–80, 186
McConnell, James, 41–2, 189
Marshall, John, 13, 95, 99, 104
Marshall, John, jr, 99, 113
Martineau, Harriet, 186
Mellor, George, 167
Methodists, 37, 73, 112, 118, 158
Mills, David, 136–9
Morpeth, Viscount (7th Earl of
    Carlisle), 75, 113
Moseley, Sir Oswald, 2nd Bt, 37
Murgatroyd, Nathaniel, 35
Myles, James, 48–56

National Regeneration Society, 113–
    14, 120
National Society, 133
Needham, Ellice, 60
Newcastle, 4th Duke of, 98–9
Newcastle, 5th Duke of, 82
New Lanark, 57–8
Newton, 83
Northumberland, 125

Oastler, Richard, 73–82, 91, 94–8,
    102, 108–18, 120, 134–6, 186
O'Connell, Daniel, 87, 169, 185–6
O'Connor, Feargus, 171
Oldham, 120
Owen, Robert, 66, 113, 114, 120,
    157
Oxford University, 146, 160

Paine, Thomas, 90
Parke, Sir James (1st Lord Wensley-
    dale), 137
Patten, John Wilson (1st Lord
    Winmarleigh), 103
Pattison, James, 68–9
Paxton, Joseph, 11
Peel, Sir Robert, 1st Bt, 13, 66, 68,
    176
Peel, Sir Robert, 2nd Bt, 84, 132,
    135, 184, 185–6
Perceval, Thomas, 26
Piecers, 22

Pilling, Richard, 170–2
Pitt, Thomas, 83–5
Place, Francis, 157–8
Plug Plot, 133, 159, 169–72
Poor Laws, 16, 20, 41, 62, 66, 70,
    78, 80, 99, 100, 132, 146; see also
    Acts of Parliament
Population, 35, 99
Porter, George, 12
Potter, Richard,
Preston, 63, 146
Price, Theodore, 68, 70
Primitive Methodists, 34, 82, 112–13
Protectionists, 82
Pudsey, 129–31
Pugin, A. W. N., 13

Quakers, 61–2, 146

Radicals, 66, 71, 73, 80, 82–3, 85,
    96, 110, 114, 116, 120, 124, 135,
    157, 184
Raikes, Robert, 22
Railways, 14, 15, 41, 54, 62
Ramsbotham, Henry, 35
Rand, John, 34
Richardson, Cavie, 105
Rickards, Robert, 125
Rochdale, 62
Roebuck, John Arthur, 56, 157
Royle, Vernon, 141–2
Rugby, 14
Russell, Lord John (1st Earl), 181,
    186
Ryder, Thomas Dudley, 136–9

Sadler, Michael Thomas, 18, 32,
    44–6, 70, 81–2, 91–2, 94, 97–102,
    104, 108–9, 113–14, 140–1, 143–4,
    172
Salford, 84
Saunders, Robert J., 161, 164
Savings Banks, 26
Scholes, 71
Scotland, 40, 46–59, 93, 96, 125, 161
Scott, Sir Walter, 13
Senior, Nassau, 146–52

Shipley, 36
Sheffield, 14, 175
Shoddy industry, 12
Short Time Committees, 71, 77, 78, 82–5, 92, 104, 108–20, 129–36, 144
Sibthorp, Charles de Laet Waldo, 186
Silk industry, 12, 68, 128, 141
Simond, Louis, 56–9
Smith, Adam, 144, 174, 178
Smythe, George (7th Lord Strangford), 41
Southey, Robert, 153
Spinners, 22, 55, 56, 58, 85, 141, 149–51, 155–6, 168–9
Staffordshire, 125
Stanningley, 71
Stephens, Joseph Rayner, 83, 118–20, 136
Stirling, William, 46
Stockport, 12, 18, 166, 171
Strickland, Sir George, 7th Bt, 97–8
Strutt, Edward (1st Lord Belper), 13
Stuart, James, 161
Styal mills, 143
Sunday Schools, 22–3, 115, 129
Swaine, Elizabeth, 35
Swaine, John, 35

Taylor, William Cooke, 37, 61–5
Thackrah, Charles Turner, 27–9
Thomas, C. E. Poulett (1st Lord Sydenham), 120, 124, 127
Thornhill, Thomas, 73, 80
Todmorden, 34, 120, 134
'Tolpuddle Martyrs', 85
Tories, 32, 41, 66–7, 73, 80–2, 96, 98–9, 110–12, 114, 118, 132, 135, 146, 170, 184
Tractarians, 158–9
Trade Unionism, 21–2, 36, 62, 85, 113, 140, 146, 151, 154–5, 157, 167
Trollope, Anthony, 59

Trollope, Frances, 59–61
Trollope, Thomas Adolphus, 59
Turner, James, 157
Turton mills, 61–5

Ure, Andrew, 124, 146, 152–7

Vickers, Joseph, 133

Wakefield, 36, 162
Wakley, Thomas, 124
Wales, 40, 125
Walker, William, 60
Walter, John, 135
Ward, Sir Henry George, 175
Warwickshire, 68, 70
Watt, James, 58, 180
Weavers, 12, 22, 23–4, 58, 83, 141: see also Handloom weavers
Wellington, 1st Duke of, 81
Wentworth, Godfrey, 36
Wesley, John, 67, 112
Westmorland, 125
Wharncliffe, 1st Lord, 158–60
Whateley, Richard, 37
Whigs, 66, 96, 98, 110, 112–13, 135, 172, 184
Whitehead, Abraham, 70–1
Wilberforce, William, 108
Wildman, Abraham, 71
William IV, King, 88, 91, 96, 106, 112
Wing, Charles, 124–5
Wood, George William, 103
Wood, John, 13, 60, 73, 114
Woolcombers, 36, 167
Woollen industry, 12, 17, 29, 36, 70–1, 87, 93, 104, 141
Worsted industry, 12, 34–6, 71–2, 74–6, 141

Yorkshire, 59, 70–80, 83–4, 92, 95, 108, 125, 133–4, 158, 165, 167, 185
Young England, 13, 14, 41–2